BOOKS BY

MAX FREEDOM LONG

The Secret Science Behind Miracles
The Secret Science At Work
The Huna Code in Religions
Growing Into Light
Self-Suggestion
Psychometric Analysis
What Jesus Taught in Secret

WHAT JESUS TAUGHT IN SECRET

A Huna Interpretation of the Four Gospels

MAX FREEDOM LONG

DEVORSS *Publications*

DeVorss & Company, Publisher
P.O. Box 550
Marina del Rey, CA 90294

Printed in the United States of America

Contents

Foreword

It was on Thanksgiving Day, 1968 that Max Freedom Long wrote to me saying, "I have been wondering for the steenth time if I could simplify Huna enough to do a little book for Christians titled *What Jesus Taught in Secret* and in it leave out the technical part and stressing the fact that only what is in the Four Gospels is according to the Code Original and trustworthy."

I urged him to begin the manuscript which he wanted to be published as a small paperbook book. It was begun in 1969 and finished in August 1970, just a year before his death at almost 81. He sent it as a special gift to me and it has been unpublished until now.

In my search and quest for more enlightenment a friend gave me the two Huna books then published, which was almost thirty years ago. Mr. Long was a courageous and open-minded scholar. I am convinced of the fundamental integrity of his character and the soundness of much of his reasoning. He was an educated and devoted man, open-minded and gentle. He lived the no-hurt, no-sin life. He was a gentleman and a scholar.

As one of his long-time students I helped him, during the last years of his life, to coordinate his more than fifty years of tireless research work in the Polynesian religion. He was prolific, with six books on Huna, four detective novels, a children's book, more than 200 research bulletins sent through the years to his 500 students over the world, and his series of lectures on Cassette tapes.

He both gave and willed me all of his work, and I am still awed by the vast amount of careful research he accomplished—"digging" as he called it for more truth.

This is an unusual and unique book. There is some reason why you are holding it in your hands. Read it with an open and inquiring mind. It is for study and a "so-old-but-new" yardstick toward understanding more fully your three selves.

Now comes an important part: As you read this quote from the Huna Vistas Bulletin, no. 97, page 5 it may not mean much and is not clear, but do not despair and above all do not give up. After you have completely finished the book, turn back to these quoted paragraphs and let them be the final ending of *What Jesus Taught in Secret*.

The Questions of the Three Selves bothers some of those who write to me. In the OUTER teachings of Christianity and some other religions, as they have come down to us, we have matters simplified by giving the man a single "soul," and many hesititate to give up that idea.

In early Egypt, and in the later Polynesian Huna, we have our familiar concept of THREE SELVES or souls, and in India the selves gradually multiplied and the manas and emotions and mind levels were treated as "selves." The founders of Theosopy sorted and tried to put the tangle in order, coming up finally with only SEVEN selves, which they termed "Bodies." This was a valiant effort to replace the TEN ELEMENTS of man, his three selves, his three grades of mana, his three shadowy bodies or doubles, and his physical body during life. Their *Atman*, or High Self, was left with only the vaguest of shadowy bodies and mana, and no effort was made to explain where these came into the picture, or why they should be left out. The mana we send as a gift to our High Selves was symbolized by honey in the Egyptian system, and *awa*, in the Hawaiian. It was the nectar of the gods for the Greeks, and in India it was the sacred soma juice which no one had ever seen or tasted, but which was still considered the drink of the gods or of the evolved soul. One gets used to the idea of the three selves and finds it very useful in explaining the modern idea of the subconscious, conscious and superconscious. It is worth the effort to make the acceptance—very much worth all the letting go and rebuilding one's background picture.

I have so many letters arriving which tell of the joy of finding at last a system that answers the many hitherto unanswered questions and which acts as a catalyst to make the valid parts of many religions fall into place neatly and with meaning. More than that, it is a workable system. We *can* get Help with our problems many times, if we just remember to ask, and pray in the right way with properly visualized ends and the sending of the mana to empower the High Selves to get to work.

Study carefully the illustrations and their explanations, for with your broader view you too may uncover another portion of the code and mystery.

In Huna Light

Dolly Ware
Owner and Curator
Max Freedom Long Library
Ware Crest Press
425 S. Henderson
Ft. Worth, Texas 76104

Introduction

I have a strange and almost unbelievable story to tell. In the 1920s, I lived in Hawaii and busied myself in my spare time writing detective stories. They were not much of a success, but in searching for plots for them, I made a study of secret codes and methods of breaking them. The detective fiction made me very much aware of any hint of a "code."

During the same period, I had begun to write on the native religion and practices of the Hawaiian *kahunas*, or priests, who had died out shortly before my time, but who had known and used some very secret methods in their "magical" practices.

Shortly after I began writing on the secret lore of the *kahunas* (which word means "keeper of the Secret"), I made a delightful discovery. I found that the SECRET (their lore had no other name that I could ever find), had been hidden behind some kind of code. Naturally, I was much intrigued and set out to *break the code*. But it was most difficult. I discovered that they had used a strange combination of words from their own native language, mingled with strange symbol-words such as "water," "grasshopper," "light," "bird," and other words which, if one did not know what they stood for, left wide gaps in the decoded meanings—holes which seemed at first impossible to fill.

Beginning with my first book on this subject, in which I told of the few provocative things which were revealed by the small part of the code which I had been able to break, I progressed by slow steps in my research. This first book (1936) was published in England shortly before the outbreak of World War II, and the few copies of it which had not been sold, were destroyed by German bombs. However, one reader who had been an English newspaper correspondent, wrote to me, saying he had once found a people in Morocco where the Secret Lore was known and used, and that he would be able to help me a little. He had studied with the head of a small tribe and had learned something of the lore— enough to help me discover the meanings of some of the most baffling word-and-code symbols. Oddly enough, these people had spoken a "special language" in discussing their religion, and from his yellowed pages of old notes, it was easy to see that this was a Polynesian dialect closely resembling the Hawaiian, but more nearly like the Tahitian.

My new friend, Reginald Stewart, had been made a blood son of the tribe's woman leader, who was an expert *kahuna*, and so had been allowed to partake of the Secret which all *kahunas* held to be so inviolate and valuable. Unfortunately, she had been killed accidentally, shortly after starting his instruction, and as no other teacher could be found, Stewart had given up and gone on to other things. But he had kept his notes and remembered much that he had been taught of the theory of the Secret, even if he had not learned how to use it in the magical practices.

After the War and after Mr. Stewart had died, I enlarged and revised my English book on the *kahunas* and it was published in the United States, under the title of *The Secret Science Behind Miracles*. It was the first of a total of six books which were eventually written on the subject.

There is no need to relate here how I attempted to gather friends about me and to test what I had learned of the Secret "magic." This is the story of the unexpected discovery that the code had been used in the writing of the Four Gospels to conceal the SECRET TEACHINGS OF JESUS.

When I became very sure that this discovery was well

grounded in fact, I was foolish enough to think that the Christian world would hail it as something of great value and importance—would welcome the news with wide open arms. I wrote letters and sent gifts of my books. I hopefully addressed a Pope and the heads of some of the Protestant Church organizations. Gradually, and to my great surprise, I began to find that the gentlemen of the cloth, whom I had thought should be the most vitally interested, would not even listen to me. They seemed to decide, one and all, and quite off-hand, that such a code in the Gospels was an impossibility, and that I must be a crack-pot. In no instance was I ever given a written word in answer to my letters and gifts of books. I was faced by a wall of silence.

Just what those I addressed had thought, I was never able to find out. It might be that they feared what I had to tell as an innovation which would threaten their accepted beliefs, or, in some cases, perhaps even their jobs.

In recent years, the churches have not been growing in membership as they had been doing in earlier years. The younger people, especially, are being educated away from the old beliefs which have long been fixed and unchanging. Fewer and fewer young people hold to the idea that the world had been created in six days or 5,004 years ago, as Bishop Ussher had figured it out from the Bible. Geology and the evolutionary theories of Charles Darwin have become too well known and widely accepted, despite the long battle of the Church to put down such troublesome new discoveries.

It is to these who are less confined by the old set of religious beliefs that I turn now for a hearing. A hearing is all I ask. I am not endeavoring to convert anyone from whatever religion he may prefer. But I do wish to tell all who will listen about the new Christianity which breaking the code has revealed. I am convinced that many thoughtful people will welcome the information which I hold to be of such value, and which I think could restore Christianity to its original, workable and helpful form.

The reader will be interested to know that the writings of Paul and others which go to make up the Acts and the Epistles, contain not the slightest evidence to show that the authors were initiates and knew the code. This, in itself, causes us to question the additions which Paul made to the pristine beliefs and teachings of the Master. When we know the SECRET TEACHINGS we find no need at all for Paul's additions which have so colored and hindered the understanding of the Gospels—which are the only records of what was actually TAUGHT by Jesus.

The CODE and its users have now been traced back to early Egypt, and we can follow the migrations of the people who used the Code Language for every day conversation, from Egypt to the island of Madagascar on one side of the Indian Ocean, and to India on the other. We find words of their special language left trailing behind as the moving tribes traveled on, past Java and into the Pacific, where they settled in uninhabited islands all the way from New Zealand to Hawaii and Easter Island. The date of the migration can be set at about the year 1 A.D., as these people brought with them many of the Bible stories, from that of the Creation and Adam and Eve through the Flood, but failed to have the slightest knowledge of Jesus and his associates. It is evident that they left the homeland before the first appearance of Christianity.

The world has reached, we hope, a final condition of stalemate in which war on an atomic scale is too terrible to be contemplated, and now is moving rapidly into what some call "The Aquarian Age"—an age of social justice and economic stability, with the several great governments of the globe gradually turning in the direction of cooperation.

But we see the churches breaking down all about us. Priests are leaving the Church of Rome in rebellion against its fixed ideas and positions, and laymen of all churches tend to draw away and seek a less dogmatic faith.

It is of the greatest importance at this difficult stage of world transition that religion be restored to its proper place in the lives of men. We have seen that we cannot agree on the rather unscientific dogmas of Christian sects. We have long disagreed with the dogmas of Islam, Buddhism and other Oriental beliefs. We need a second coming of Christianity, with the secret teaching of Jesus cleared of the hindering dogmas which have attached themselves to it, and a return to the true teachings of the Master as they are restored to us by the breaking of the Code. We have now before us a pure and high religion of finest moral values. We can once more have a faith that can be fixed on something very real—on Something which will help us and answer our prayers if we learn to pray correctly.

As we go along with this study and learn the things which were withheld from the masses of his time by Jesus, we will meet the false beliefs which were added as an accretion and be able to lay them aside in favor of a far more logical and satisfactory set of beliefs—the set that Jesus left to us as our bright heritage, and which can now be ours if we are able to open our minds and hearts to it.

(Signed)
Max Freedom Long.

CHAPTER 1

The Almost Unbreakable Code

After almost 2,000 years, the *key* to the coded mystery teaching hidden in the Four Gospels has been discovered. All down the years it had been suspected that there were such hidden teachings, for Jesus had said, "unto you it is given to know the mystery of the kingdom of heaven; but to them that are without, all things are done in parables."

Once the Code was broken and the "mystery teaching" was laid before the world, a wonderful NEW LIGHT was cast on the teachings of the Master. It was seen that only a small part of the teachings had ever been allowed to escape into the hands of the ones who were "without"—the uninitiated.

But for the initiated, such as were the Disciples, there is today, as there was at the very beginning of Christianity, a wealth of strange, new information. The true meaning of many obscure passages is disclosed as is the secret of the PRAYER OF THE MIRACLE. There has been added the knowledge of another and more wonderful Salvation—one of still greater promise.

Of great value to us is the CORRECTION of many mistakes which were made through the lack of understanding of the true meaning behind the outer teachings. We can now begin to clear away the false doctrines which arose because of the misunderstandings, and win through to a new, vital and workable religion.

Codes come in a variety of forms. Most of them are based on a mechanical something, and with a "code book" one can "decode" messages. The more difficult codes are those based on a little-known language, as was the unbroken code used in the recent war with Japan in which groups of Navajo Indians were stationed on ships of war and set to visiting by wireless telephone from one part of the war front to the next, speaking in the Navajo tongue with their friends, and, in the course of the conversations, passing on such information as that a Japanese officer of the High Command would be flying at a certain time into a certain place, and might be shot down by our airmen. The Japanese, not suspecting that such conversations were being held in a known language, searched in vain for a clue to the method, and, failing to find it, suffered several signal defeats.

The code which was used in the Gospels was such a code. It was simply the use of a special language in which to compose the original documents before translating them into languages common to the Greeks, Hebrews, and other people in the Near East around the year 30 A.D.

But, to make the code more difficult, certain words were used which had several quite unrelated meanings, and, unless one knew these key words and what they stood for, one could hardly get started with the breaking of the code.

An example of a code is to be found in a language which was not used for a code, but still baffled all who tried to read its messages. This was the Early Egyptian. It was written in hieroglyphics and as no one knew the ancient and long dead language, no one could read the papyrus scrolls or inscriptions on the many monuments.

At some very early time in Egypt, there appeared a people, not many in number, but who spoke a language of their own and who had learned to use it as a spoken code.[1] (They had no writing.)

These were the ancestors of the Polynesians, as we shall see in good time. Their language was ideal for the purpose of mak-

1. A technical and detailed account of the Code and all the proofs and explanations, together with a dictionary of the Code and symbol language may be found in my book, HUNA CODE IN RELIGIONS.

ing a code to conceal their greatly valued secrets of what we may call "magic".

The language was made up of words, many of which, like the later German when compounding roots to name scientific items in chemistry, were made up of several combined roots. Each of these words had one, or as many as fifteen, different shades of meaning, and, in addition, the roots themselves had special meanings and several alternate meanings.

Added to the common words which could be used for the code, there were pressed into service a few common words, as has been said, such as grasshopper, bee, water, light, bird, web, etc., which had special meanings which if one did not know them, effectually prevented the breaking of the code as a whole. The early Egyptians had their kahunas or initiates, and in the hieroglyphics we find the more common code words, but that was all. The complicated meanings could be expressed only in the special Code Language.

Once the code is understood and one has the language before one to use, all is very simple. But until that time, the secret meanings remain very safe.

Perhaps I should pause here to give a little information about the early Egyptian language and writing. The system of writing seems to have been originated in the Nile Valley, and is found from earliest times as hieroglyphics or little pictures representing the things mentioned in the writing. Papyrus reeds were beaten into a pulp and joined to make papyrus or paper, on which the scribes wrote or rather drew, with ink and pens made of split reeds. In time the use of an alphabet was developed, some of the glyphs being used to represent sounds, but as the vowels were left out and had to be supplied by the reader, the precaution was taken of adding to the end of a word or line one of the old pictures to represent the thing under discussion. There were both alphabetic symbols used and phonetic or syllabic glyphs. About five hundred characters were used in all, and much later the glyphs were more and more simplified in the drawing until they become a flowing type of near-script called the Demotic.

For years the Egyptologists were unable to translate the many hieroglyphic or other writings found on monuments and written on papyrus, sheets of which were pasted together to form a scroll. Then the Rosetta Stone was found, and on it a royal decree written in the old languages and also in the newer forms and in Greek. It was from this priceless Stone that there came eventually the ability to translate the "Book of the Dead", which had for centuries on end been placed in the coffin with mummies, also inscriptions on statues, temples, and monuments.

All the inscribed material of the First Dynasty was of the hieroglyphic type, and dates back to about the year 3300 B.C. As time passed, the shortened or hieratic script came into use, and there is a wealth of writing in this form dating from about the Twelfth Dynasty and the so called New Kingdom. Gradually, thanks to invasions of Semitic and Arab peoples, the language changed. The consonants were mispronounced, strong consonants giving place to weak, and these in turn disappearing entirely; other changes produced bilateral from trilateral roots. The tendency, together with periphrastic instead of verbal conjugation, continued to the end. In time the whole language became lost and the Coptic which was written with Greek letters arrived by about 900 B.C. The degraded graph writing, the Demotic, passed with the passing of the old language, and by the fourth century A.D., no one knew the old language or how to read even the Demotic script. The Coptic was a dialectic form of the old language, but resembled it so little that it was almost no help in showing how the words of the early writings were to be pronounced.

After the translation of early inscriptions was made possible by the discovery of the Rosetta Stone, translators were forced to supply the vowels in words, and many got left out entirely.

In order to understand what Jesus was so much engaged in teaching, we need to know what he believed and how he came by his beliefs. As the same CODE was known and used in Egypt, we must look here for the first appearance of the great SECRET into which Jesus was initiated. By breaking the CODE as it was used in Egypt, we will make ourselves ready to examine the hidden teachings in the Gospels, and we will find that they were not something new, but very old, and, very well matured, thought out, and placed in an amazingly ordered and logical system—a system that included the Psychology of man and his relation to Higher Beings, as well as religion.

Just how old the SECRET is, it is impossible to say, but the evidence seems to suggest that it was hoary with age at the time we first pick up traces of it in the picture writing or hieroglyphics of the Egyptians. The time may be 5,000 years or more back, or 3,000 years before the time of Jesus. Where the system of beliefs and practices originated, is a mystery. Some say it was brought to early Egypt from a lost Atlantis— from some great but vanished earlier civilization. But of one thing we can be quite sure, it was a fully developed and completed system at the time when we begin to find traces of it coded into the earliest Egyptian inscriptions.

The Secret Was Unique

The SECRET was unique in that it was housed and preserved and passed on from one initiate to the next by means of the *special language* which I am tempted to call "The Language of the Code." This language was not reduced to writing, so far as I know, until modern times, and then in far Polynesia by missionaries. In its very early home, it was the common tongue of the ancestors of the much later Polynesians. Originally, they seem to have been few in number and divided into 12 little tribes. Each tribe, in later years, in their new homes in the Pacific and in Madagascar, developed a slightly different dialect, but kept the code words unchanged because they had simple and basic meanings. Eleven of the tribes have been recognized in their new homes, but the twelfth (perhaps the "Lost Tribe of Israel") seems to have moved overland to what is now Morocco (where Reginald Stewart found them).

We do not know why the people who spoke the code language every day resisted the temptation to allow it to become a written language. But at no time in Egypt or the Holy Land was it written, and if some initiate wanted to record some of its secrets, he translated the code words into another language which had evolved a written form.

For this reason we find the code words only in translation in earliest Egypt. One word, the most sacred and important in the religious system of the Secret was the same in Egyptian and in the code. It was the word "Ra" or (as rendered by the Hawaiian missionaries, "La"). It means LIGHT.

THE SECRET MEANING OF THE WORD "LIGHT"

The SUN was very important to the Egyptians from the first, and their outer worship was a mixture of sun worship, and moon worship. Over this they spread a blanket of totem gods which took animal form, each part of the land favoring one animal god or another, and all of them borrowing gods back and forth. Very soon they gained a fair knowledge of the stars and their movements, and soon busied their priests with astronomy, mapping the heavens and making fresh gods out of the stars and star clusters. They learned to set the time of the yearly flooding of the Nile by the movement of the stars, and, like the neighboring peoples of the Tigris and Euphrates valleys, became very well civilized for a people of their day.

The Egyptian scribes developed into no mean artists. They formalized their little glyph pictures to some extent, and drew them with singular sameness on papyrus paper or, cut them into stone to make lasting inscriptions.

The neighboring peoples, who had no papyrus paper, turned at an early date to the use of wet clay to write upon, later baking or drying the clay to make tablets or cylinders. As clay is not too good for drawing, they quickly developed an alphabet and represented letters by making a series of wedge-formed marks on the clay, the cuneoform or "wedge" writing. The Hebrews, while in captivity in Babylon, adopted this writing method, changed it a little to fit their own language, and were soon writing with ink on skins which they dressed to make parchments. These, like the Egyptians with their thin paper, they glued together to make rolls, and in due time the rolls or scrolls contained parts of the Old Testament as well as other documents.

That the Hebrews had made early contact with the "Keepers of the Secret"—the *kahunas*—is evident from the fact that their word for "priest" is "cahun," even today. The Egyptians and the people of the code language, however, were the only ones to use the same word for "sun" or "light," *ra* (or *la*). For the Egyptians who were not initiated into the Secret, their one meaning for Ra was "the sun," but for the initiates, who understood the code word *la*, a set of several meanings was known.

An Example of the Code Being Used in the Gospels

Let me give you an example of the code as used in the Gospel of John. We have it translated back from the Greek (which was used in the Holy Land in the days following the writing of the Gospels) into the Hawaiian. The translation was made by the missionaries in the years soon after 1820, and is fairly good, considering the fact that they failed to translate code words correctly. Here is a sample of what may be a document very similar to the one which was written by the Disciple John, supposedly after the death of Jesus.

(John 14:6.) *"Olelo mai la o Iesu ia ia, Owau no ka ala, a me ka oiaio, a me ke ola: aole kehahi e hiki i ka Makua, ke hele ole ia ma o'u nei."* ("Jesus saith unto him, I am the way, the truth and the life: no man cometh to the Father, but by me.")

Here we find John giving us almost the whole of the secret teachings in a nutshell. In the words, "way, truth and life" he has used the simple words which stood for almost the complete system of religion (and Psychology), which Jesus taught in secret to those who were his chosen—to his disciples.

It is well as we start looking into the coded teachings, to note that when Jesus said, "I am" or "I give you," he was in reality saying, "I offer you this teaching or enlightenment." In his person he could not by any stretch of the imagination *embody* the items named in the code words. He TAUGHT THE SECRET MEANINGS of them.

In the language used for the code, there was no "I AM," it gave us simply "I," as in the passage *"Owau no ka ala,"* which translates literally, "I" plus the affirmative particle, *"no,"* and the words *"ka ala"* or "the way." In translation we supply an "am" which is *not* there and *not intended in the code meaning*. We should read, "no man cometh to the Father but by me," to carry the code meaning of "through what I teach."

Unfortunately, the direct statements, deprived of the coded meanings, were the ones passed on in the OUTER teachings to the uninitiated, and these statements became the dogmas of Christianity. "Only through me" and "In my name," replaced the inner teachings and froze the major meaning of Christianity into strange and distorted form. If I had succeeded in breaking the code a century earlier, I would have been unable to understand what I had found. I would have had to await the *discovery of the subconscious* mind by Psychology, and the postulate of a *Superconscious Mind*.

The Missionaries to Hawaii, in 1820, could not possibly have understood what the native *kahunas* were trying to tell them in the years when they worked with the wisest of them as helpers, to translate the Bible into Hawaiian. *The natives knew the subconscious, the conscious and the Superconscious*, and had names for them that dated back for 5,000 unchanging years. Psychology, our infant science, had not yet made even a beginning.

The native word in Hawaiian which translated "grasshopper" had a double meaning, the alternative being THE SUBCONSCIOUS SELF of man. This word was used in ancient Egypt, and with the same secret DOUBLE MEANING. The Superconscious was *LA* or to make it more sacred *LAA* in Hawaiian, and the same word in the form of *RA* was used in Egypt for as far back as records go.

It is amusing to note that the missionaries settled on the word for the CONSCIOUS MIND to use in making a translation of both conscious and subconscious and added "Holy" to it to get a word for "God." This word meant, in Hawaiian, THE SELF WHO CAN TALK (Uhane). It is also amusing to read the Bible in Hawaiian and find that God is called the equivalent of *The Holy conscious Mind Self (Uhane Hemolele)*.

One of the discoveries which startled me most was that these three parts of the consciousness of man were known to the Keepers of the Secret. At first I thought it as impossible, but eventually I came to accept the fact and to go on from there in the breaking of the code. I also came to see in time that the original SECRET taught that these three parts of the "mind" were not parts of each other, but three separate things or selves which were joined in the closest possible association in man. Jesus even taught that the LIGHT Self was so close and intimately attached to man that it might be called "The God Within."

Jesus was a great Psychologist. He knew all that modern Psychology knows and teaches, and much more that we, as moderns, have not yet caught up with. Psychology still has not more than guessed at the fact of the Superconscious Self. And, as late as 1914, Professor Munsterberg, who was the great "authority" on Psychology at Harvard University, proclaimed, "The story of the subconscious mind can be told in three words: there is none." We are still at least 50 centuries behind, and if Holy Church had been able to hold its own in the battle to stay in the Dark Ages, we would still believe that the earth is flat and that man has but one self or soul. This despite the fact that in Christianity men have been reciting endlessly, "In the name of the Father, the Son and the Holy Ghost—three in one, world without end. Amen."

Freud gave us the *subconscious* part of the human trinity. Jung postulated the *Superconscious*, but the Behaviorists in Psychology still strive valiantly to deny us even the *conscious mind*. Man gives up nothing with such reluctance as some idea with which he has been indoctrinated early in life.

CHAPTER 2

The Early Training of Jesus

Until we come to understand the early training of Jesus and what it was that he learned and what initiations into the lore of the Secret he experienced, before he was ready to take up his ministry, we cannot hope to gain an insight into the things that he taught in secret.

Unfortunately, the initiates who wrote the four different coded accounts of the life of the Master, the Four Gospels, did not write for "those who were without." They appear to have been trying to record in writing and in code, such parts of the hidden lore as were of greatest value. They took it for granted that anyone who read the accounts would KNOW the basic principles upon which the faith of Jesus was founded—would at least be already familiar with the same Egyptian beliefs as was the one of whom they wrote so carefully.

We might say that there was an unwritten set of gospels, these handed down only by word of mouth to make advanced students ready to understand the coded secrets preserved in the WRITTEN Gospels.

For example, the Master spoke freely and openly of the Father, of himself as the Son, and of the Comforter or Holy Spirit. Not once did he pause to go back over what had gone before or to explain the subconscious self or the conscious self. He spent all his energies driving home the hidden truths which lay behind "the mysteries of the Kingdom"—the

10

Kingdom and the Father, if you please. In that direction lay all the Salvation that was possible, and he was teaching his Disciples to understand it and to win through to it.

THE BASICS OF THE CODE

In my own efforts to break that strange Code, I should have been baffled by the Gospels had I not already been immersed for years in a study of the SECRET as found in Polynesia and in the records of Ancient Egypt.

It was the custom in olden times to teach secret things by word of mouth and through elaborate dramas of initiation. Egypt had great halls where the *mystery plays* were staged and the neophites taught. In later times the same was true of Greece, and Jesus, in his turn, was busily engaged teaching, living and exemplifying the TEACHING in his "mystery of the Kingdom of Heaven."

So sacred was the old lore held that down the years no one has ever revealed what the mysteries actually were—what was said, taught, and dramatized. Many guesses have been made, and we have decided that there were several such Mysteries, but no initiate ever told in writing what was actually taught—that is, not until the coded Gospels were written.

A very strange thing seems to have happened. After the four versions of the Gospels had been put into writing, they were either stolen or given by choice to the uninitiated. We may never know which. It may have been a test to see if the apparent and open outer meaning could be spread abroad while the coded parts remained secret and within the order.

Paul was one of those into whose hands the writings appear to have fallen. And, as he had never known Jesus during his ministry and before his death, and as he did not suspect the presence of the code, he was greatly puzzled. But he seemed to have realized that in the Gospels he had found something of the greatest value, for he set about filling in the parts which had not been plainly stated. And in doing so he caused the genuine and coded teaching to be lost almost entirely.

WHAT JESUS MAY HAVE LEARNED IN EGYPT

There is a tradition that Jesus traveled and studied in Egypt and other foreign lands in the years between the time we see a brief glimpse of him as a boy of twelve, talking with the learned men of the Temple in his own land, and the beginning of his teachings. Nothing at all is said of the years that followed until the story continues with his first contact with John at the age of about thirty. We read in some accounts that as a baby he was carried to Egypt to be safe from the order of Herod to kill all of the first born male children of a certain age, and so learn that it could not have been a journey too difficult to take at a later period in his life.

Or, we may guess that he was instructed by other men who had learned the lore of the Secret in Egypt. But when I began to study the parables of the Kingdom of Heaven, there were many things which caught my attention as being familiar to me in my own study of the very ancient Egyptian beliefs and practices.

I remember wondering about the parable of the sowing of the seeds, and the other parable of the mustard seed which was the smallest of seeds but, when sown in a field, . . . ''when it is grown, becometh the greatest among herbs, and becometh a tree, so that the birds of the air come and lodge in the branches thereof.''

The Egyptians made much of seeds, and I found a drawing of a mummy from which grain was growing. They were said to have believed that man followed a life cycle similar to that of grain in that the seed grain must become dormant, be planted in the ground, and then sprout and grow into more grain. Man died and was dormant as pictured in the mummy, then his spirit took on new life, and as in the case of grain, grew into a new form of life and being.[1]

1. If you would care to check on the Egyptian items I am mentioning, go to a good library and ask the reference department to let you have books on the beliefs and practices of Early Egypt, also books on the early hieroglyphics. Budge has written many fine books on the several phases of the early culture and you are sure to find him well represented. Alvin Boyd Kuhn has several books dealing with the early Egyptian beliefs, (and he draws heavily from Massey in his book,) but for our studies his ''The

In the Egyptian I found that the "spirit" was symbolized by a bird, and in the parable it was said that birds of the air came to lodge in the matured mustard plant as in a tree. As the only mustard plants I knew about were seldom more than a few feet tall and would hardly be large enough for a bird to lodge in, I wondered whether or not there might be coded something in the passages.

In the hieroglyphics of the earliest dynasties of Egypt, I found that the "spirit" of man was represented by a bird, a form of stork, but, what interested me most was that in the famous "Book of the Dead," there were often pictured three such birds, crowded one into the other to represent man's spirits as being three in number. I knew that the Polynesians believed in three spirits or souls, and Jesus spoke of a trinity of spirits in his Father, Son and Holy Spirit. But this did not seem to indicate just the higher or god-like spirits above man, but also to include the physical man, Jesus, as the SON.

Turning to Massey and his great books, I learned that "Son" was *ISU* in the Egyptian, which became "Jesus," and which meant "son." In this case the FATHER of the "son" was NOT Ultimate God, but a lesser god who had been a man. He was Osiris, husband of a lesser goddess, Isis, and father of the son, Horus. These three were worshiped in Egypt and legend said they had lived on earth, just as Jesus did, and that they could very well duplicate the Holy family, Joseph, Mary and Jesus. What was most important was that they acted as a TRINITY to watch over the faithful believers, and that the mother, Isis, matched the "Comforter" rather well.

To get back to the clue of the three birds or spirits, found in the Egyptian writings and having an echo in Christianity,

Lost Light" and his most recent book, "A Rebirth for Christianity," will be best. Massey's books contain wonderful studies of the Materials of which I write, but are now hard to find. His "Egypt, the Light of the World," is recommended. If a copy of the Andrews, "Dictionary, Hawaiian-English," of 1865 is available, it will furnish proof of all word meanings. My first book, "Secret Science Behind Miracles," is basic for the study of the beliefs of the Polynesians and for a general survey of world religions. My later book, "The *Huna* Code In Religions," is for the reader who wants all the information possible on the subject now being handled in popular and briefer form.

we come to the same idea as already found in my study of the beliefs of the Hawaiian *kahunas*. The bird was also the symbol of a spirit to them. It could stand for one or more spirits, and they called the human body the place of roosting, which suggests the birds residing in the mustard plant tree.

The Hawaiians held as part of their secret knowledge, the fact that there were, attached to the human body, three spirits, one of whom was called the Father, or just the "Parental Spirit", suggesting the Mother as well as the Father in the combined spirit or entity. (We cannot have a Father without a Mother.) The peculiarity of the secret belief was that the three spirits were so closely bound together that they resembled just one "self."

It was to be seen that the outer teachings gave the masses the simple belief in one soul, and we see that this was held more or less the world over, but that one soul was known by initiates to be made up of three parts, and we of modern times now have the subconscious, the conscious, and the Superconscious parts of mind. The question arises as to just how united or separate these are.

Jesus taught two parts of the soul in his Father and son, quite openly, but did not go farther than that except to say that some spirits of the dead returned and obsessed the living, and had to be cast out. From the kahunas we learn that the subconscious and conscious parts of the soul can become separated after death, at least for a time, and that the "devils" who must be cast out vary greatly in their nature. They counted obsession done by the subconscious alone, or by a combined subconscious and conscious, or by a conscious part of the soul alone. The Superconscious was thought never to be involved in such activities, but helped under certain conditions to do the casting out.

The strangest and most baffling code clue in the earliest Egyptian secret beliefs was found in a strange symbol drawn as just the uplifted hands and arms, and breast, as if in prayer or supplication. Budge translated this glyph *"ka"* and said that it meant "the human double or aura." Others spelled it *"khu,"* and we are at liberty to supply the vowel and make it *"aka"* which is the Hawaiian, and which has the same meaning—the double or shadowy body.

In the cartouche or what might be called the name plate of Pharaoh Menkure of the 4th Dynasty, we find the sun pictured at the top of his seal to indicate that he was a divine ruler, a Son or Ra, the sun or Light God. Underneath is a crown, to signify his royalty, and below that are THREE of the glyphs for the double.

In the secret lore of the kahunas, we find the explanation of the THREE elements. They believed that each of the three selves lived in its double, and that the subconscious and conscious spirits blended their doubles and lived in them during physical life but both interpenetrated the living human body. The Superconscious Spirit also had a double, but it did not live in the body. It lived above it, and was always connected to the man by a "silver cord" which acted as a means of communication and allowed the man to send his prayers at any time to the Father Self. This last mechanism was of the greatest importance. Jesus was at great pains to explain it in his secret teachings, and it was the most important single item in his instructions given for the making of the prayers which could bring the Superconscious Self into action and produce miracles. The superior POWER of the Highest Spirit of the human Trinity was recognized in the Egyptian, as well as the Hawaiian systems, and was stressed by the Master. Later, we will consider at some length just how such a prayer is to be made. The part played by the *"ka"* or *"aka"* double is most important, and without it, no prayer of this kind was thought to reach the Father Self.

The Egyptian seers appeared to be afraid that this very important part of the man might be overlooked, for they had a second set of glyphs to name it and still conceal its secret significance. This symbol was the SHADOW of the man. The glyph was one little umbrella for each of the three doubles; sometimes we see all three drawn together in illustrations. Their name for "shadow" was "khaibit," and in the Hawaiian their word, *"aka"* did double duty, also meaning "shadow." We inherit the idea in our "shades" who haunt the earth, as "the shades of the dead."

Budge and others who tried to explain the strange beliefs of the early Egyptians, became all tangled up in the "shadow" and the "double." They learned from the old writings that the shadow of a king was something venerated and held very dear; not only in life, but after life when in the mummy stage and in the heaven world. During life, in Egypt and in Polynesia, the shadow cast on the ground by the person of a king or chief was not to be stepped upon under penalty of severe punishment. As we know, this was only symbolic of the real shadowy body, but the double was more than the shadow on the ground, it was a lasting and wonderful thing, and there were three doubles.

The telephone line from the shadowy body and the subconscious self, who lived in it, was made of the same substance as the double. It was so shadowy that it could not be seen except with clairvoyant vision. It was so important that it had its own symbol, that of a strand of SPIDER'S WEB. The strand was also thought of as a "thread," and in India the "sacred thread" was worn as a symbol around the neck of a Brahmin—a symbol of his close connection with a Superior Being. The idea was enlarged to include threads strung with beads, the beads symbolizing prayers being sent along the shadowy thread from the subconscious to the Superconscious.[2]

The kahunas believed that the thread to the Father, from much use, became a CORD, but that filmy threads connected people and things with a person.

The Egyptians made much of the idea of the threads and cords, and the glyphs for them were of several kinds, always showing a thread and no more, even if bent or knotted. Their prize glyph, however, and one that later was used as their letter "h," showed the threads interwoven to make three shadowy bodies, one above the other, and all tied neatly together. The sign of "power," an extended arm, when laid across the sign of the three shadowy cords was the hieroglyph for "to rejoice" and we gather that this refers to an answered prayer, which brings "rejoicing."

The bead as a symbol is as old, it would seem, as the symbol of a crown or halo above the head is to stand for the Superconscious or "God Within," (who is really above the man, not

---

2. The American Indians also spoke of going in the "shadow body" after death to search for a loved one on the "other side."

within him). The Egyptians made much of the symbol of the thought-form as the "seed" (as Jesus preferred to call it) and as a "Ball." Their prize symbol was the dung beetle who rolled a ball of dung, laid an egg in the center of it, and left it in the sun to hatch. This they even made into a god, Kepera, "the Roller." This was the famous scarab, and it was made into images of various sizes and placed with the mummy in its sarcophagus. The god represented the ball of the sun, being rolled across the sky. Altogether, it was most important and . . . greatly misunderstood. It was even thought to play a large part in the creation of the globe of Earth, and in the resurrection of the three-part man into the heaven of Amenta.[3] The little balls of various substances which were used for beads, all represented the pattern ball of the beetle, and, in the secret meaning, the thought-forms of the prayer.

In the language of the kahunas, they spoke of a ball as a thing of the night, or subconscious self (the benighted one) as in contrast with the fine light of day, the symbol of the Superconscious. In other words, the prayer was a ball of thought forms sent from the night of the dense physical world to the light world of the Father.

One of the outstanding parts of the Secret was the knowledge that only the subconscious self had the ability to use telepathy, and as all prayer had to go to the Superconscious TELEPATHICALLY,[4] the prayers had to be made into thought forms and given to the subconscious to transmit to the Superconscious. The making of the Prayer of the Miracle was based in large part on this mechanism.

The subconscious or animal self, was called the *ba* by the Egyptian initiates. It was the self whose abode was thought to be in the heart, and it was the self who lived in the *ka* or invisible shadowy body. The human body was considered

3. The mechanism of telepathy is well illustrated by the beads on their thread, and stand for the sending of thought-forms, as beads, from one person to another.

4. The thought-form belief is common in India even today. The use of beads as the symbol known in the secret teaching, however, is lost. The idea of prayer beads seems to have been borrowed from the Buddhists by Persians and Arabs. Mohammedans soon were using them, and eventually Christian monks took to their use in keeping count of the number of prayers they had recited.

apart from the heart-soul, and was called the *khat*, and the combined subconscious and conscious spirit selves, in their respective shadowy bodies was called the *khu* and this was thought of as a shining, luminous, intangible form having the shape of the physical body.

The symbols of the Egyptians, when it came to the parts of men, ran to insects, and the grasshopper was the symbol of the subconscious, the spider the symbol of the cords or threads of invisible material drawn from the double of the subconscious, and the bee the symbol of the conscious self. But the Superconscious was too sacred to be symbolized by an insect, and a bird was used, in Christianity the dove, which has become our "dove of peace," while the major symbol for it was LIGHT or the Sun.

In my early search for the suspected presence of the Polynesian beliefs in the literature of Early Egypt, the grasshopper proved to be a prime code clue. It was *unihipili* in the Hawaiian, and had a double meaning: a grasshopper, and the subconscious self. The Hawaiian language is so constructed that several little root words, each with as many as a dozen different meanings, could be added together to make a complete word to name something. In this case the roots of the word for the subconscious self told what it was, what its nature was, and described its relation to the conscious mind self.

But its symbol, the grasshopper, was needed to tell what it was good for or could do. In order to understand why the grasshopper had been chosen for the subconscious self symbol, we must note a rather amusing thing. The insect, when caught, will produce from its mouth a flow of brown WATER, and water is the symbol of the human vital force, called *mana* by the kahunas.

The subconscious self and it alone, has the ability to manufacture from the foods we eat and the air we breathe, our basic vital force or power. Once made, it stores it in the body for use, and it shares it with the conscious mind self, who may be said to live as a guest in the bodily house, and who has little to do with the bodily processes. The Superconscious self must also be supplied with the vital force if we ask it to work with the dense materials of the lower plane of living and make miraculous changes in matter, or simply make the "answers to prayers."

In the Bible and in Egyptian literature we read usually of the locust, as it was the most impressive form of the grasshopper and caused the most trouble. We read in the Gospels that John lived on locusts and wild honey, and this is pure Secret symbology. The locust was the producer of water, which was the low or basic form of vital force, and the product of the bee is HONEY, which is the symbol of the vital force when given to the Superconscious when we pray. The bee, as the symbol of the conscious self, does not indicate that the honey is made by this self, but tells the initiate that the conscious self is involved in the process of prayer, and that it makes the thought forms of the prayer and instructs the subconscious to SEND VITAL FORCE WITH THE TELEPATHIC PRAYER TO THE SUPERCONSCIOUS.

The Egyptians called the vital force *sekhem*, and this covered all forms of it, whether used by one self or the other. The word translates, "power." The kahunas of Hawaii called it *mana*, and it was known by the initiates who were instrumental in forming the coded parts of the Bible. We translate it from the Hebrew as *manna*, but recall that no one was ever sure what it might be, although it was said to fall from heaven and become food. This was an apt symbol for the answers to prayer sent from the Heavenly Superconscious. The symbol of water is also used in the Old Testament and we find Moses and his people in the desert suffering from thirst. He uses his staff and strikes the rock, producing a miraculous flow of the symbolic WATER.

Jesus turned water to wine, giving us the secret information that the basic or low mana has to be used to produce the higher form of it represented by the wine.

The Greeks borrowed the idea from the Egyptians and their legends told of the ambrosia which was the drink of the Olympic gods, this being a drink replacing the honey, but just as tasty. In India they have written from ancient times of the "soma juice" as the sacred drink, but no one now knows what it was.

When the Master cured the blind man, he used saliva, following the typical method of the grasshopper, and made mud with it to place over the blind eyes to bring about the miracle of restoration. In the story of another healing, the man was instructed to go to the Pool of Siloam and when the Angel troubled the waters, to bathe in them. The waters were the mana used by the Father or Superconscious, who used the basic force sent by the subconscious. Isaiah, who was an initiate, if we are to judge by his use of the code, speaks of the "desert" to be made to become "pools of water." In other words, our deserts where we suffer, will be transformed by sending mana to the Father in prayer.

The Egyptians were vague in their symbols of the flow of the mana to the Superconscious, but not so the kahunas of their day and of later Polynesia. In their language we have the clues to the mechanics of prayer, and, in brief, it is that the vital force or basic mana FLOWS LIKE WATER, and can be sent along the shadowy cord to the Superconscious as electricity along a telephone or power wire. The sages of India knew the mechanism at one time, and called the cord or threads of shadowy material *nadi*,[5] or tubes. The kahunas often used the symbol of water flowing through a tube in this connection. For our study, it is enough that we know that the basic vital force is sent by the subconscious to the Superconscious.

The mana of the subconscious self was basic and there was lots of it needed to move the physical body and do a day's work. But this grade of the "power" also had another use. It

5. *Nadi* also meant a current or flow of vital force. The Secret was known in the earliest Yoga of India, but as time passed, was almost completely lost. The wise men of India, once the basic knowledge was lost, began to experiment. They finally evolved an elaborate system called Kundalini Yoga in which the bodily force was raised by meditation from the lower end of the spine, up through the nadi *tubes* on both sides of the spinal cord (itself a tube), and made to pass out through the "Door of Brahm" or top of the head. Where it went from there was not too well understood, but the force, called "prana" instead of mana, wa supposed to go to some Higher Being and cause results of a miraculous nature. The uninitiated were warned that they might kill themselves if they misused this power or did not understand it. It was not used for healing, as it was believed that the Law of Karma dictated that man suffer out his illnesses to pay off old debts.

was the force behind mesmerism, which is the hypnotic power of the subconscious self. It can accumulate a large over-charge of mana by an act of its lesser will and by heavier breathing. This charge can be projected to another person and even render him unconscious for a time. The magicians of old knew and used this force. We rediscovered it as "mesmerism"[6] in France just before the birth of the new and still incomplete science of Psychology, but when we discovered hypnosis, a little later, mesmerism was all but forgotten. Hypnosis is the same power projected and used by the conscious self. It takes the mana from the subconscious and with an extra supply in hand, adds the force to the sug-gestion which it makes silently or aloud, and we all know of the results it obtains.

The mana, when sent to the Superconscious, is accepted and changed in some way so that it becomes magically power-ful. It can be used to cause changes in physical matter, as we see in instantaneous healing which sometimes occurs. Jesus called on the Father for such help, and taught, "Not I, but the Father, he doeth the work." The slower changes brought about by the Father come through changes made gradually. If one asks for some change, the old and undesirable condi-tion must be torn down and the new built in its place. We will go into this later and at length, as it is of great importance that the process be understood so that we can do our part in send-ing the Superconscious the thought forms needed to use as "seeds" and the daily water of mana used to water the seeds and make them grow.

Little jars of wheat or other seeds were often found in the burial chambers of Egypt as reminders to the mummy that human life was like seed life, and that after a period of rest and burial, like the seasonal planting of the seed in the ground, there came new life and the resurrection.

6. Neither the symbol nor the word for mesmerism was found in the Egyptian, nor for hypnosis. But the kahunas of the time undoubtedly knew and used both in that far land. They carried their knowledge with them to Polynesia, and there used the idea of the "seed" in a phrase, "to plant a seed or thought in the consciousness of another person." They had several words for "seeds," apparently with the intention of making sure that if one word lost its secret meaning, another would remain to replace it.

CHAPTER 3

The Gospel Story Opens With
Much Coded Information

We have now seen that in his early training, Jesus had learned the great SECRET, perhaps from the initiates of Egypt. We have seen that in this system of belief and practice there was a knowledge of the three selves or spirits of the man, the three shadowy bodies which survived the death of the physical body, and the three vital forces, one grade for the use of each self, but all derived from the basic mana made by the subconscious self. With the physical body, this makes ten units, not too complicated to understand with a little study, but sufficient to explain many things which have been mysteries to our Psychologists and Religionists up to this time.

John, who leaned more to the Greek terminology of the day, opens his account with, "In the beginning was the word, and the word was with God, and the word was God." In the Greek we find *Logos* used for "word", and around this there has been built the belief that the Logos was just another name for God.

We have to go back to the Egyptians to help get the matter straightened out. They theorized about Creation, and taught that Ultimate God created the universe and the Earth as a thought or plan, and that, in order to make the thought material, he produced a lesser god to "speak the word" and cause the creation to become materialized. In fact they made a God of the Word.

This matches the teaching that the thought forms or plan of a condition or event, made by the man as the first step in prayer, is a creative act, but to materialize the plan, a lesser god is needed to "speak the word," and this points to the Father or Superconscious.

The kahunas were more definite in their concept, and in their language from which the Code was made, we find "word" translates, (*hua olelo,*) or "seed made with the voice."

THE NATIVITY is not mentioned in some of the Gospel accounts, and contains little of the code except to tell us that Jesus was the son of a *carpenter,* and from this we know that he had received his training as a kahuna.

It is not stated openly that Jesus was himself a Kahuna, but in the later story of his life every piece of the coded information tells us that he was one, and of the very highest grade.

In the Samoan dialect of the Polynesian or Code Language, the word for carpenter translates *KAHUNA* and the code in the roots tells us that he was a *lighted or enlightened self.*[1]

THE STORY OF JOHN THE BAPTIST as told by some of the Gospels, leads us to believe that his coming was foreseen by Isaiah and that he was fulfilling the prophecy:

Mark, 1:1. ". . . Behold, I send my messenger before thy face, which shall prepare the way before thee . . . the voice of one crying in the wilderness, Prepare ye the way of the Lord, make his paths straight."

The original is to be found in Isaiah 40:3, and I use Fenton's translation:

A Voice cries in the Desert, "Prepare the Lord's path: —And straighten for passage the road of our God! Raise the valleys, and cut down each mountain and hill. Make the crooked path straight, and the rough places smooth. The Lord's glory unveiled, let all see it at once, As the Lord's mouth has said."

1. The word is *la-au* which means "wood" or a kahuna who works with wood. The root *la* is "light" the root *au* is a "*self*". We still use the term enlightened soul or being. The tradition of masters is strong in India and is being adopted in the Western World. Jesus was counted as one of the masters by the early Theosophists.

THE CODE MEANING OF "MESSENGER" is a multiple one: "true, spirit, power, (mana) energy, force, God."[2] This makes John also a kahuna and one initiated into the Secret, as would be fitting for one announcing the coming of the Messiah and calling on the people to repent their sins and make ready for the great event when the Great Leader would appear and bring in the new day, with God taking over the rule of the earth and administering justice, with, of course, the aid of the Messiah.

THE CODE MEANING OF "THE PATH." As we have seen, "path"[3] in the code language is very important. The word translates, *path, or way* and contains the root for "light" which tells us where the path leads, to the High Self. This is the shadowy cord leading from the subconscious self, to the Superconscious Self, and it can be blocked by our guilts, fixations and by spirits who exert an evil influence over the man. This is the "passage" or road "to our God," and to "make crooked paths straight" the symbolic "mountains and hills" and "rough places" must all be removed. The removal process is coded in John's call for giving up sins and repenting, then his mystic cleansing away of all the obstacles blocking the path with the baptism with water. The water is the code for mana, and mana was used to drive out "devils" or obsessing spirits. "Our God" is the Superconscious Self—the only place where the shadowy cord or "path" can lead.

"THE LORD'S MOUTH" is an important addition by Isaiah to his coded information about the shadowy path to the

2. *Io.*

3. *A-la* has several significant meanings to be used as part of the code.

a. "To rise up," symbolizing the rising of the mana along the connecting aka cord to reach the High Self as the sacrificial gift from the lower man.

b. "To anoint." In this meaning we see the gift of mana as something used to anoint or "make holy and sacred." The initiate who knows the secret of the path and its uses, is an "Anointed One" or a "Christed One."

c. "To awaken." In this we have the symbolical meaning of awakening one to understand the fact that there is a High Self. It is the same as "enlighten," which is to dispel "darkness" or ignorance of the verity of the High Self.

Superconscious. "Lord"[4] translates in the code *the one who directs others,* and from the roots we get the meaning of the special "Breath Rite" on which the sending of the prayer to the Superconscious is based. This consists of heavy breathing to accumulate the surcharge of mana to send to the Superconscious and accompany the thought forms of the prayer. The "mouth" tells us plainly that the breathing and speaking to form the prayer go together. Isaiah was no mean composer of coded lines to pass as prophecies. Whether his prophecies were valid or not, we do not know, but it is to be seen that John and Jesus took them to be true and that the time had arrived for them to "come to pass."

We have already seen the code use of "The Way, the Truth and the Light," as used in the Book of John. Matthew, Mark, and Luke do not make use of these code-word-symbols in telling the story of John the Baptist, nor does John include the story of Jesus, after his baptism, going for forty days into the wilderness to fast, be tempted of the devil, and to come back into the habitable world to begin his ministry, which, as we shall see belongs after the resurrection. However, they all agree that Jesus was recognized as the Messiah and a man who needed no baptism with the water of mana to open his path. The High Self in the form of a bird—a dove, descended upon him to complete the symbology, and a voice said, "This is my beloved son, in whom I am well pleased."

John has Jesus at once begin to choose his disciples, but the other narrators delay this while they have him return home to announce in the temple, after reading the prophecy of the coming of the Messiah from Isaiah, that he was, indeed that great personage and was ready to lead and take up his ministry.

Luke, 4:14-21, reads: (Fenton's translation)

4. *Ha-ku.* Used for "Lord" and symbolized by a bowl in Egyptian hieroglyphics. The source "from which all blessings flow." NOTE: The careful student will be interested in the fact that the kahunas who helped the Hawaiian Missionaries to translate the Gospels, selected the word *kuamoo* to use for "path" in one place when trying to give the exact meaning of Isaiah. The word also means the backbone or spinal column, and we see here the suggestion that the kahunas also knew of the "tubes" which the sages of India called "*nadi.*"

"Jesus then returned to Galilee with the power of the Spirit; and his reputation spread throughout the whole of the neighborhood. And he taught in their synagogues with the approval of all. He afterwards came to Nazareth, where he had been brought up; and, as his custom was, he entered the synagogue on the day of rest. And standing up to read, there was handed to him the roll of the prophet Isaiah. And opening out the roll, he found the place where it is written, 'A spirit of the Lord is upon me, by which He has appointed me to tell good news to the poor; He has sent me to heal the broken-hearted; to proclaim freedom to the enslaved, and restoration of sight to the blind; to set at liberty those who are oppressed; to proclaim the year honored by the Lord.'

"And having rolled up the book, he returned it to the attendant, and sat down. And the eyes of all the synagogue were fixed upon him. Then he began to say to them, 'To-day this Scripture is fulfilled in your hearing.' "

"A spirit of the Lord" gives us our first bit of code. We know that the High Self is a spirit and "Lord" is symbolized in the Egyptian as a bowl which becomes the "cup that runneth over", or the cornucopia and horn of plenty as the bowl is tipped and the "seeds" or prayers in materialized form are poured out. The code word[5] means *the prayer* and *the one to whom the prayer is sent*, which tells us that the High Self is the Lord. When we speak of Jesus as "the Lord," we are referring only to his High Self, and must remember that Jesus often spoke as if he were his own High Self or the Father.

"The poor" does not mean simply those of no worldly wealth, as the outer teachings seem to indicate. In the code the word means *those who are not rich*[6], or the ones who have no extra mana-water and do not know how to send it to the High Self to "water the seeds" of their prayers when they have been sent. The "rich," in contrast, are named with the code word for[7] *much water*.

"The broken-hearted"[8] gives us the root meaning of those who have *breaks in their low selves*, which is something we will

5. *Ha-ka.*   7. *Wai-wai.*
6. *Ilihune.*   8. *Eha-eha.*

explore later. It means that their line of contact with their High Selves has been broken or blocked by convictions of guilt or by fixations, even by obsessing spirits or "devils" of the Gospels. These are also to have the good news brought to them to bring them out of their darkened condition.

The "enslaved"[9] are those who are *bent, crooked, held captive,* and this repeats the code word for the "broken-hearted," again with the information that those obsessed and controlled by evil or devil spirits are to be rescued. We have nothing to tell us that the Master ever tried to empty the prisons of his day.

The "blind"[10] are those whose *sight is darkened.* This covers all who have not yet come to know the Light or High Self.[11]

The "year honored by the Lord" means only the beginning of a new year and does not relate to the secret teachings. It is, rather, an indication that Jesus was convinced that he was the Messiah, so long expected, and that he would soon begin to lead the people in such a way that the rule of God in the world would be realized. This is a very important point for us if we are to understand what lies behind the crucifixion and the transfiguration—both items of much significance in the inner teaching. As Jesus was reading a coded passage from Isaiah, we know that he recognized in that prophet, who had been dead for 700 years, another initiate into the lore of the Secret.

In the accounts of the beginning of the teaching and ministrations of Jesus, as given by Matthew, Mark and Luke, only the latter contains the story of the reading of the scroll

9. *Pio.*
10. *Makapo.*
11. For convenience sake, let us drop the clumsier terminology of the subconscious self, conscious mind self and Superconscious Self, and substitute the terms, low self, middle self, and High Self, as I have done in my earlier books. This casts no shadow of opprobrium on the low self, but simply describes its place in the evolutionary scale. It is the least evolved but a most useful member of the triune team of selves. I will put the code words from the Hawaiian in the footnotes for a time, and go ahead with the explanation of their application to the passages we will study, putting the code meanings in italics.

which immediately showed that Jesus continued in his own person the prophetic tradition of the Messiah recorded in Isaiah.

The writer of the Book of John made no mention of the claim that Jesus was fulfilling the prophecy of Isaiah, and leaves out the story of the rejection of Jesus by the people of his home town. However, the tradition is brought to mind in John 4:44 where Jesus is quoted as saying, ". . . a prophet hath no honor in his own country." He might well have said that a teacher of the inner truths could have no hearing from those unable to understand what was being laid before them.

When Matthew wrote his account of the life of Jesus, he referred constantly to the prophecies and wrote of various events, "This came to pass in order that the prophecies might be fulfilled."

After Luke's little drama in which Jesus announces himself as the one to fulfill the prophecies, we are told that his doubting listeners refused to believe him to be what he claimed. To them he was just the son of Joseph and Mary. But they had heard of the miracles of healing which he had been performing and so demanded that to prove himself he repeat the miraculous performances before them and "show signs." For some reason, usually said to be because the townsmen lacked faith, Jesus could not comply, and, as a result, was about to be stoned and thrown over a cliff, but he managed to escape.

The question of whether Jesus was or was not the expected Messiah had not been settled. The code shows us that Jesus had not the slightest thought of becoming a leader in the military sense but one to lead the Jews to a position of world domination through spiritual leadership. The common people failed to understand this. In their eagerness to have the Messiah of earthly power arise, they flocked around Jesus, listened to him when he taught in parables, and marveled at his power to heal and to cast out devils. Meantime, the learned Jews and their religious leaders watched with increasing indignation.

The Good Tidings or message proclaimed by Jesus takes us back once more to Isaiah and the prophecies, then to John the

Baptist as the first in line of those coming to fulfill the prophecies. Like John, Jesus also taught, "Repent ye! The Kingdom of heaven is at hand!" And, to try to explain what he meant, Jesus at once began to use parables. These had an outer as well as an inner meaning, and, as the inner meaning was understood only by those of the "chosen," the prophecies were again brought to the fore.

In Isaiah, 28:9-13, we read: "Whom shall he teach knowledge? and whom shall be made to understand doctrine? them that are weaned from the milk and drawn from the breasts. For precept must be upon precept, precept upon precept: line upon line; here a little and there a little: For with stammering lips and another tongue will he speak to his people. To whom he said, This is the rest wherewith ye may cause the weary to rest; and this is the refreshing: yet they would not hear. But the word of the Lord was unto them precept upon precept, precept upon precept; line upon line; here a little, and there a little; that they might go, and fall backward, and be broken, and snared and taken."

The implications in this prophetic passage, when the "weaned from milk" is mentioned, is that the old and mature were the only ones who could understand the Huna secrets. Even these more advanced individuals when chosen and instructed, would have to be taught "precept upon precept" and with the use of the words of the code language—this resulting in the teaching "with stammering lips and another tongue . . ." The ones who were to listen, however, were not all to be able to accept what was offered. Some were to "fall backwards, and be broken, and snared and taken." The symbol of the "snare" stands for all the obstacles which prevent the "path" from being opened to the High Self. Fixations and the influence of evil spirits also come under this symbol.

Jesus knew the Code and was able to fulfill all the hidden elements of the prophecies of Isaiah. As we shall see later, he expected the coming of the end of the world, and to see the "heavens unrolled" and himself seated beside God, judging the resurrected dead and the living alike. Happy in this belief, he pursued his ministry.

THE CALLING OF THE DISCIPLES comes almost immediately in all of the accounts. The number of them is given by all as twelve, and this may or may not refer back to the early Eqyptian preoccupation with the twelve signs of the Zodiac, one of which was marked by the sign of a fish, Pisces. From the point of view of the Code, the fact that the fishermen were selected by Jesus to be his disciples, has an immediate meaning. The name for "fisherman"[12] in the Code Language contains two familiar roots, the one for *light* the other for *water*. We know the symbol of "water" for the mana, so gather that Jesus proposed to teach the disciples to know the High Self as the "light," and also the nature and use of mana. There is also a play on the roots of the word that makes the meaning of "foul water", so we may also see that he proposed to clean up the fishermen and remove from them their guilts and fixations, perhaps even obsessions.

The code word for "disciple" translates *to inhale* plus *mana*.[13] And as we have seen, heavy inhalations of air help accumulate the large supplies of mana used in prayer and also in casting out devils and in miracles of healing. The disciples may have been trained to supply extra mana when Jesus was performing miracles of healing or when casting out very strong and evil spirits.

John would seem to say that Jesus selected his disciples at once, then began his ministry of teaching and healing, taking them along in his travels and having the opportunity to teach while he demonstrated by showing how healing was done. But in the other versions of the story, Jesus performed many miracles before calling the disciples.

In the outer teachings the healings are said to have been brought about by Jesus, using his own power or by calling for the help of the Father. Quite another set of meanings appear when the code words are inspected and at the same time the Huna healing philosophy studied. To the kahunas the usual cause of illness was the "blocking of the path" to the High

12. *La-wai-a.*
13. *Hau-mana.*

Self. To bring about healing, the "blockings" were removed, then the High Self requested to accept a goodly supply of mana and use it to do the actual healing. Jesus explained, in John's account, "Not I, but the Father, he doeth the work." In cases where the contact with the High Self had been "blocked" by a sense of guilt or by fixed false ideas held by the low self, there was the need to cleanse away the blocks. Jesus sometimes said, "Your sins are forgiven you." Or he might say, "Be cleansed." This cleansing or forgiveness[14] in the language of the code means, "*of the light*" or "*to restore the light*," this symbolizing the opening of the shadowy cord or "path" to the High Self so that mana can be made available and can be used to bring about healing.

In cases where evil spirits fasten themselves on victims, they prevent the contact with the High Self and so keep the Father from casting them out. Jesus healed the obsessed by casting out the evil spirits, using the mana in the Mesmeric or Hypnotic form to force out the spirits, after which he instructed the victim to accept the "cleansing" and to give up his own evil ways so that his bodily "house" would remain clean and contact kept with his protecting High Self.

The healing of a leper was described in detail. (Mark, 1:40-42.) "There came a leper to him, beseeching him, and kneeling down to him, and saying unto him, If thou wilt, thou canst make me clean. And Jesus, moved with compassion, put forth his hand and touched him, and saith unto him, I will; be thou cleansed. And as soon as he had spoken, immediately the leprosy departed from him, and he was cleansed."

The code word for cleansing or "make clean"[15] in the healing sense is excellent code and translates from its roots *to unite* and *to cleanse*, so we see that the man had his path opened and was once more united with his High Self as a part of the healing action. The same root has the meaning also of "a cluster or bundle," this being the symbol of the cluster of thought-forms making up the mental picture of the man in the healed condition—this picture being sent to the High Self on a flow

14. *Ka-la.*
15. *Hui-kala.*

of mana to enable it to make the physical changes resulting in the healing. The word for "will" is also code[16] and means to *desire greatly*. The first root[17] has the meaning of *to be right, fitting and proper*, also of *to permit*. These meanings all apply directly to the making of the Huna prayer for healing. The patient must be "made fitting or proper," through the cleansing rite that reopens his path to his High Self. The one making the prayer must also have a very strong "desire" for the healing to be brought about, and on this hinges the Huna belief that all emotions, such as desire, are generated in and by the low self in cooperation with the middle self. If the low self does not desire to have a prayer answered, it will not do its part in the work and the effort is useless. The same root word also has the meaning of "*to die; to perish*," and this is a code way of saying that the life force or mana is much used up in enabling the High Self to perform instant healings.

In verses 30 and 31 we read, "But Simon's wife's mother lay sick with fever; and anon they tell him of her. And he came and took her by the hand, and lifted her up; and immediately the fever left her, and she ministered unto them." The key code words here are "lifted up," which is the usual symbol for "lifting up" the mana and the thought-form picture of the prayer for healing to the High Self.

Mark, 2:3-6, relates the story of the healing of the man suffering from palsy. Jesus said, "Son, thy sins be forgiven thee." This tells us that the "cleansing" was given, and the fact that the man suffered from palsy gives the clue as to what needed to be cleansed away to open his path to the High Self. Palsy is a word that has the code meaning of *the seat of the low self consciousness in the abdomen.*[18] The low self harbors fixations and hidden feelings of guilt that must be removed so that the path can be opened and healing take place.

(NOTE: The kahunas, after leaving the Near East to settle in Polynesia, used a baptismal ritual with water as part of the cleansing of a patient, and if the one to be healed could make

16. *Make-make.*
17. *Make.*
18. *Lo-lo.*

amends to persons who had been hurt by him this was demanded before the cleansing rite was performed and the healing was asked for in prayer. In the code in the Gospels, the elaborate details of such rituals were impossible to describe, but the ones who were initiated needed only to be given hints in code words to remind them of the entire process. Baptismal *water* is *mana* in some form, symbolized or ritualized, "holy" or not.)

Mark, 3:1-4, gives us unmistakable information about the need for the heavy charge of mana to be sent to the High Self in order to bring healing. We read that a man with a "withered hand" was healed. The code word for "*withered*"[19] has the meaning of "*dried out or wilted*," which symbolizes the lack of mana, the symbol for which is "water." The man's affliction had, supposedly, come about because he had lost his full contact with his High Self and had let it "dry out" or lack a sufficient amount of mana to protect him, the lesser man. Jesus corrected this and with the mana supplied, the healing was made possible.

The need for mana to empower the High Self to heal is touched upon again in Mark, 5:25-30 in which the woman with the long-standing "issue of blood" touched his garment and was healed. The "virtue had gone out of him" at the touch, so he knew what had happened. The word in the language of the kahunas for "virtue" is *mana*, and here no code is needed, simply a statement that the mana had been taken from him so that he felt it and so that the healing was accomplished.

In Mark 6:38-42 we have the account of the healing of the damsel of whom he said, "the damsel is not dead, but sleepeth." In healing her he took her by the hand, and "hand" has special code significance for the word for it means to divide mana.[20] In other words, one accumulates a surcharge of mana, and through the hand gives a portion of it to the patient and another to the High Self so that it can help with the healing. Holding her hand, he "raised her up, and she was

19. *Maloo.*
20. *Manamana-Lima*

healed." When he commanded her to "arise" he used the code word which means *to lift up*[21] and which symbolizes the lifting up of the mana to give it with the prayer for healing to the High Self.

Passing from healing to the control of wind and sea by Jesus, we come to the familiar story of the "rebuking of the winds" and the command to the sea to be still. The later kahunas in Polynesia practiced a similar control over wind and weather as well as over fish and turtles in the sea, so as we go on in the story of Jesus, we also find that he exerted his powers to bring about the quieting of a storm on the Sea of Galilee.

In another miracle he told the disciples, who were fishing, but had not made a catch, just where to throw their nets, and the result was a "miraculous draft of fishes." We have there the word "nets"[22] and are reminded that when he called them to come and follow him, they "left their nets." This word has the code meaning of "*a snare*" and the symbolic meaning of something that blocks or breaks the path or shadowy cord to the High Self. The same word has the meaning of to *anoint*, so we see the implication that to have one's path cleared and to be put into full contact with the High Self is in some way connected with the rite of anointing which was practiced in Egypt as well as by the Jews. The Greek word means "to be Chrisomed or Christed—to become a Christ or High Self."

To take or catch a fish[23] has also the code meaning of *to stretch a cord from one place to another*, or *the final completion of a work*, or *white and shining*.

The miracle of walking on the water is related in Matthew, Mark and John, but not mentioned in Luke. It is possible that what the writers were telling in the code had a direct bearing on the large amount of mana needed to perform a major miracle, and the Disciples may well have assisted in accumulating and sending the mana to the High Self of Jesus or of the ones to be healed.

21. *Iluna.*
22. *Upena* or *Koko.*
23. *La-wa.*

Only John relates the story of the miracle of turning water into wine. In this there are a few significant meanings hidden in symbols, and, knowing as we do that water was the symbol of mana, and that miralces were done by asking the Father to perform them, the accumulation of a surcharge of mana is seen in the filling of the six water pots "to the brim." The servants who filled the pots were then ordered to "draw out" and "bear unto the governor of the feast," the latter symbolizing the High Self, to whom the surcharge of mana is sent in all prayers. The water is then revealed to have become wine, a symbol of the change which the High Self makes in the lower mana to use it to bring about changes in physical matter, these usually resulting in healing, but in this story the water was changed to wine (honey to Egyptians, ambrosia to the Greeks).

John, in 9:1–10, tells of the restoration of sight to a man who had been born blind. An important bit of philosophy was touched upon openly in the question asked by the Disciples, "Master, who did sin, this man or his parents, that he was born blind?"

The belief in reincarnation is plain here, as the man could not have sinned before his birth unless in a previous life. Jesus replied, "Neither hath this man sinned, nor his parents: but that the works of God should be made manifest in him." The Huna belief was that man, having to incarnate in an animal body, shares with all life on the physical level, the chance that by some accident of circumstances the imperfections may replace the intended and normal course of life. Here, the outer meaning was given in the statement that the man had been allowed to be blind in order that the power of God might be exhibited in the healing.

Jesus spoke of himself as the lesser man of the low and middle self combination in verse 4: "I must work the works of him that sent me, while it is day . . ." The word, "day" is the symbol of "light," or the High Self and so we see the "work" is to be done only when the High Self is united with the lesser selves to perform the miracles.

In verse 5, Jesus speaks as the High Self united with the lesser man, saying, "As long as I am in the world, I am the light of the world." (Read, "I teach about the Light.")

The account continues in verse 6, (already mentioned) telling how Jesus spat upon the ground and made clay of the spittle and earth. The code word for "spittle"[24] has, from the roots, the meaning of *to stretch out or reach the hand*, which is a symbol of the inner act of reaching out to contact the High Self, as in prayer. It is similar to the "stretching of the cord." Another root symbolizes the heavy breathing and accumulation of mana to be sent to the High Self when it is asked to perform a miracle.

The blind man was ordered to wash the clay from his eyes in the "pool of Siloam," which was noted for its healing powers. The high mana of the High Self is indicated in this washing, because it caused the changes in the physical matter of the eyes to correct the condition of blindness. (The Huna belief appears to have been that the shadowy body of the low self duplicates every part of the physical body and acts as a mold surrounding it. If the blind eye was to be restored, the substance of the eye would be dematerialized for a moment, then materialized once more to fit the shadowy mold, the latter always being perfect, even if some "accident" in the physical level has injured the physical counterpart of the mold which forms at birth and survives after death. The man who loses a leg during life, reaches the other side of life in the spirit world after death, clothed in his shadowy bodies—one for each self. As the shadowy body of the man remains perfect, the leg is replaced and is normal in so far as a spirit is concerned.)

In the inner teachings of the Gospels, as revealed by the Huna word code, the mechanics of healing are only partly described. The kahunas of later times in Polynesia were the physicians and healers and used various methods. Some specialized in the use of herbs known to have medicinal value. Some used a form of massage which included manipulation of the joints, much as Chiropractors do today.

24. *Ku-ha.*

There were kahunas who specialized in counteracting spirit attacks and spirit influence exerted over the living. Other healers (there were several grades of healing kahunas), laid on hands and sent their mana, with the mental pictures of the normal condition, into the part of a patient which had gone wrong. Instant or nearly instant healing was performed with the help of the High Self of the kahuna (or, in some cases by the help of the High Self of a good spirit who could be called upon by the kahuna for help, much as modern healing is accomplished by the "guides" of some Spiritualists).

A kahuna's patient was, in fairly modern times, examined to learn whether or not he had a sense of guilt resulting from hurting others. If such a sense of guilt were found, the patient was sent to make amends for the hurts. If they could not be made to individuals, certain acts such as fasting or making gifts to the needy were prescribed by the healer, the idea being that the patient must come to believe that he had righted the wrongs, and also that physical acts and self-sacrifice would impress the low self that its man was now cleansed of guilts and ready to be healed by the High Self through the agency of the kahuna.

The actual healing by the kahuna often took the form of the preliminary cleansing (*ka-la*) of the patient with a sprinkling or baptism with water while the kahuna affirmed that the last taint of guilt was washed away and the patient was fully cleansed. The invocation was then made to the High Self, and often the kahuna laid his hands on the patient. The mana needed by the High Self for the healing was usually supplied by the kahuna when the prayer for healing was made. The prayer was often repeated three times, word for word. Where instant healing of a broken bone was done, the amount of mana needed was not great. Natural healing was caused to take place with greatly increased speed.

In cases such as the healing of the eyes of the man who had been blind from birth, as told in the account of John, more mana would be needed to dissolve the eye tissues momentarily and rebuild them in the perfect shadowy mold of the eyes, as normal eyes. In modern Spiritualism, where materialization and apports are being worked for in a seance,

it is customary to form a "circle" of several people, these join-
ing by clasping hands, with the medium acting as the focus
of the "power" generated. Without knowing it, the sitters can
often supply enough mana for a spirit to use to produce the
desired phenomena.

Individuals differ in the amount of mana or vital force they
normally have or can produce. In seance records we find that
some mediums can, without a circle to draw from, produce
physical phenomena such as "direct voice," apporting,
transportation of objects from place to place, (even of
themselves) and levitation. The extravagant use of mana,
however, often depletes and weakens the medium.

From the coded Huna in the Gospels, we are given to
understand that the High Self Father of Jesus performed all
the miraculous "works." But it is possible that the High Selves
of the Disciples also had a part in major miracles. The
kahunas often spoke of "the Great Company of High Selves"
and believed that on the higher levels of life there was often
a close association of groups of High Selves. In bringing about
world or national changes, these groups may work together,
drawing mana from the lower men as needed. The code word
for "company"[25] means "to break up," and this suggests the
Huna belief that the future events which have been constructed by the High Selves in the shadowy substance to fit
the actions of men on the lower level, may be "broken up"
when prayers are made and events are to be changed for the
better. We can only speculate as to the amount of supervision
given by the "Great Company" or the many "Great
Companies."

Although the outer teachings in the Gospel are that Jesus
was accustomed to forgive sins, there is little to show that the
ones he healed were first made to make amends for the sins
of hurts done to others—but it is safe to conclude that the healing work, as taught in the inner circles, included the kahuna
method of cleansing. The sins of failure to obey the religious
instructions of the priests of the Church are not actual sins in
terms of Huna. But any act that hurts another was, to the

25. *Poe.*

kahunas, a sin of the kind for which amends had to be made directly or in kind. Because the code shows so clearly the elements of Huna belief and practices in the accounts of the life and work of Jesus, it is permissible to conclude that forgiveness for the sins of hurting others was actually given only after amends had been made, even if the details of the steps taken to bring about the cleansed condition of "restored light" were too many and perhaps too complicated to set down in the coded portions of the writings.

To understand the inner teaching concerning the nature of SIN and the part it plays in healing or the lack of it, we must consider three code words for "sin." One general word means *to hurt another*[26] with act or thought or word. This is the only sin that counts in the secret lore. Men have added the host of sins which come from failure to perform the outer rituals of the Church, such as not attending mass regularly or going to confession. Around SEX there has gathered a great array of taboos and prohibitions. Paul was especially implicated in the formation of this list of sins. Even farther back we have the Jewish literature and from it learn of the sins of sex, and in modern times we are confronted by the amazing theory that Adam and Eve committed the first great sex sin and that from that time on, all men are cursed by that "original sin" and must perish in hell if not fortunate enough to accept the "salvation" supposedly offered by the sacrificial death of Jesus on the cross.

Two other code words have root meanings which tie them together in their naming of sin and the description of what sin really is[27]. The first of these means, *to miss the thing aimed at* or, as the phrase is used in the Bible, "to miss the mark." The roots give us first *the accumulation of mana* and second, *the sending of it to the High Self*—the failure of this operation being the "sin." The final code word[28] repeats the failure in its roots the first of which means *to waste water or mana* and the second *a space between*, the "space" being the removal of one from working contact with the High Self in prayer.

26. *Ino.*
27. *Ha-la.*
28. *He-wa.*

In Mark 2:4-12, we have Jesus offering an alternate healing command to the man stricken with palsy. One is, "Son, thy sins are forgiven thee." The other is, "Arise, and take up thy bed, and go thy way into thine house." The forgiveness of sin is "to restore the light." The "arise" is code for sending the mana "up" to the High Self while praying for healing. The outer doctrine of the Church, and the priestly rite of confession and forgiveness falls far short of the fuller meaning of the inner teaching, but is excellent if the person asking forgiveness is also made to do penance—which is similar to the Huna demand that amends be made for hurts done others.

The miracle of the multiplication of the loaves and fishes is given in all four of the Gospels, and no code words were used. However, the open symbology of the several incarnations needed to perfect the man are pointed up in the account of the "Twelve Baskets" filled with what was left after the multitude had been fed.

Only Luke tells of the miraculous draft of fishes. In this incident there are no new code words used.

The walking on water episode, as related by Matthew, 14:25-26, tells us that the Disciples mistook Jesus for a spirit, and the word used as code for "above"[29] means, from the principal root, *a shadow* or *shade*, and so gives us the symbol of the spirit body which is as old as early Egypt and which we discussed earlier. It was part of the man, both when alive and dead.

The ability of Jesus to change himself into spirit form and appear to others has been counted by some as miraculous, and with this may be classed the ability to vanish in some way. Luke, in 4:28-30, tells how the angered citizens of Nazareth tried, after Jesus failed to heal or "show signs" in his home village, to take him to the brow of a hill outside the town "that they might cast him down headlong. But, he passing through the midst of them, went his way."

The implication is that he was able to make himself invisible, or that he left his body and went with them, as a visible spirit for a time, then vanished, passed through the midst of

29. *Maluna*. Principal root, *malu*.

the crowd and went his way. The code in this passage hinges on the opening words, "But (aka) he, passing through etc." The word *aka* is used for "but," and is, in one secondary meaning, the "*shadow*" or "*dim outline of a thing*" which is the symbol of the shadowy body one uses after death, or when out of the body during life, as a spirit or apparition. It may be that the coded suggestion given here and in the account of walking on water were both intended to lay the background for the scenes in which Jesus, after the resurrection, appeared before the Disciples in a fully materialized spirit body.

In Spiritualistic circles there sometimes is to be found a medium who can produce healing of the miraculous kind. In the years beginning with 1962 there were occasional reports of the healing produced by a Spiritualist in the Philippine Islands some miles in the back country from Manila. His name was Eleuterio Terte, and he was photographed and his work observed as he prayed, laid his hands on his patients, and often performed operations such as the removal of an appendix, with no visible instruments or incisions. The healer attributed the help given him to God, but, as he was known to be a Spiritualist, it is probable that he acted as a medium and furnished the mana while good spirits who were in contact with their own High Selves, actually did the miraculous work.

Similar reports of "Psychic Surgery" and spirit healing have come from various parts of the world in recent years, especially from Brazil, where Spiritualism has attracted many, despite the opposition of the Church, and where there is a hospital given over to spirit healing.

A glance at any of the magazines published for Spiritualists will show that there is a considerable number of mediums who advertise and who attempt to send their spirit friends to any part of the world to answer calls for healing ministrations. The results, of course, are often disappointing, and it may well be that without the path to the High Self of the patient being opened and amends made for hurts done others, the spirits find healing either difficult or impossible or not lasting.

CHAPTER 4

Evil Spirits Or "Devils"

We have considered the nature of Jesus, and have seen him speaking as a man as well as a High Self. We have also examined his teachings concerning the "kingdom of heaven," not as a place but as the High Self and its higher level of evolutionary progress—as the Place of Light, and as the Light itself.

We have seen that man is a triune being, made up of three spirits, and that each of these is at a different level or grade in the evolutionry School of Life. The low self is seen to be the cause of most of the "sins" of greed and cruelty, also that it often gets the wrong idea about something and clings to it with stubborn purpose, so that these fixations or complexes may prevent the better-reasoning middle self from setting the low self right on troublesome points. In addition, to the fixed and irrational ideas of the low self, to which it reacts too strongly at times for the good of the man, there is another cause of trouble, the influence of the spirits of the dead. These spirits are the "devils" which Jesus cast out, and it is most important that we consider what Huna and the code can tell us of the matter.

The belief that evil spirits can and do obsess, or influence in varying degrees, the living, is as old as history, and together with mediumship, can be traced back to Totemism. There is no need to argue that there has been such a belief down the ages, but on the other hand, there is no escaping the fact that such a belief is accepted by only a few in modern times, even by those Christians who feel that every word of the Bible is divinely inspired and so must be correct.

In my book, THE SECRET SCIENCE BEHIND MIRACLES, I have given the details of the Huna beliefs covering spirits of five kinds and their survival after death.

However, it may be worth pausing here to explain again that most spirits are made up of their own normal three selves. These are usually good. But there are also spirits who, because of guilt feelings or fixations in life have a "blocked" path to their High Selves and so, in death, remain evil and predatory. These learn to exert hypnotic control over some living victim and to force upon him their evil emotions and desires. They steal his mana or vital force to keep themselves hypnotically strong. They vary in degrees of badness and they may influence their victim in different ways. In some cases they obsess the man completely and take over the body, pushing out the rightful middle self. This may result in a complete change in personality in the man, or, if the low self is also thrust out and the spirit's own low self enabled to take almost complete control of the body, the man becomes so changed that he is insane. Obsessional insanity accounts for most of those victims who are so badly bothered that they have to be hospitalized, but there are a great many whose obsession is so slight that they can carry on fairly well. The majority of the slightly obsessed do not know what causes their emotional explosions and strange and unaccountable hates and fears, or strange bodily ills. Many of those who are treated by psychiatrists for the removal of fixations are, in reality, victims of spirit influence.

There are certain people in this world who are naturally bad. These often seem to invite evil spirits to come to influence them and share their lives. Unless these people give up their evil, and wish to have the spirit influence removed, nothing can be done for them. Our prisons are filled with these victims who share their vital force with spirits, called "eating companions" because they feed on the mana of the hosts. But a good person who wishes to be set free can be helped.

In our long research work into the Huna System, my Associates and I have found that there is a way to discover whether a person is obsessed slightly or greatly, and whether his path is blocked by fixations. The method is based on Psychometry and is called "Psychometric Analysis". Once the offending spirits are found, they can be driven out. Fixations can also be removed. Some day it is hoped that prison parole boards will take advantage of this form of testing to find out whether a prisoner is safe to be paroled or will go back to a life of crime if released. Such individuals should be protected from themselves and the public should be protected also.

Unfortunately, the kahunas who inserted coded passages into the Gospel scripts did not give us many instances of obsession and the casting out of the evil spirits. Had more instances been given, we might have gained through the code a much fuller understanding of the methods to be used to drive away the spirits and heal the victims.

We read in Luke 11:14-26: "And he was casting out a devil, and it was dumb. And it came to pass that when the devil was gone out, the dumb spake: and the people wondered." (From the Huna angle this evil spirit was one who had taken complete control of the victim and had prevented him from speaking. The spirit may have been a dumb individual during its earthly life and may have brought this affliction with it so that the victim became dumb when under full control.)

"15. But some of them said, He casteth out devils through Beelzebub the chief of the devils. 16. Then others, tempting him, sought of him a sign from heaven.

"17. But he knowing their thoughts, said unto them, Every Kingdom divided against itself is brought to desolation; and a house divided against a house, falleth. 18. If Satan also be divided against himself, how shall his kingdom stand? because ye say that I cast out devils through Beelzebub. 19. And if I by Beelzebub cast out devils, by whom do your sons cast them out? therefore shall they be your judges. 20. But if I with the finger of God cast out devils, no doubt the kingdom of God is come upon you."

The outer meaning of the above passages is clear, but it is apparent, when we begin to apply the code and translate the words into the code language, that the writer was giving inner or hidden information on the nature of obsession by evil spirits.

After death the three selves or spirits of evil people often become separated because of the actions of spirits who have been influencing or obsessing them. These lonely spirits may be of the low self or middle self sort, or the two may stay together but cut from their own High Self.

These are the "divided" spirits, of whom the symbol is found in the phrase, "A house divided against itself." The low self, when separated from its middle self reverts to the animal and has not the power to speak with words. Such was the "dumb" spirit which Jesus cast out.

The code word here is found in the *"finger* of God,"[1] the finger meaning *to divide* and this division being symbolized by the division of the fingers into five on the hand. The hypnotic force or mana is "divided," or given by the low self to its middle self for the latter's use. This force is used to control and direct our own low selves, and may be used also to cast out an evil spirit, always asking the High self to help and to get the offending spirit back to its companion self. In Spiritualistic circles the good spirits who work with the medium as "Guides" are often called upon to take such spirits and care for them so that they will cease to bother the living and go on with their progression on the other side of life.

The code word for "divide", as used in the passage quoted,[2] gives from the the roots the meaning of *to break or cut, as a cord*, which tells us that an evil spirit has broken its contact along the shadowy cord to its High Self, or had it blocked. There is also the meaning of *a company, usually not over four*, but the word may cover a "legion" of obsessing spirits such as is described in later passages.

Jesus, as a fully initiated kahuna, would certainly have been well trained in the art of using his psychometric sense to

1. *Mana-mana.*
2. *Moku-aha-na.*

enable him to know what the nature of an obsession might be, and then to project an overpowering hypnotic force to drive out the evil spirit or spirits.

Our doctors refuse to believe in spirits, but still use the old word "obsession", and try to drive out the "something" by shock treatments which makes the patient's body an uncomfortable place in which to live. But the spirits often return after the treatments have been discontinued. Some of the insane are almost totally taken over by evil spirits, as we have said, but the many schizophrenics who suffer from "split personalities"—which is only partial obsession—can be helped with the proper treatment from a person versed in the methods used by Jesus and the kahunas.

Mark and Luke tell the rather long story of the Gadarene swine. It relates how Jesus and his disciples came upon a wild and insane man who lived among the tombs and could not be bound even with chains. The "tombs" show that he was obsessed by the spirits of dead people. The spirits in the man recognized Jesus for the Son of God and begged to be let alone, but were ordered to come out of the man. They then begged to be allowed to enter the bodies of swine which were being herded near at hand, and were given permission to do so. The swine rushed into the water and were drowned. The healed man, later, asked to be allowed to follow Jesus, but was told to return to his relatives and friends.

There is little coded information here, but the spirit gave his name as "legion," and from this we know that several spirits had taken over his body. The fact that the spirits could enter the bodies of swine, suggests that many of them were separated from their middle selves and were low selves.

Continuing with the discourse on evil spirits, we read, Luke, 9:24-26: "24. When the unclean spirit is gone out of a man, he walketh through dry places, seeking rest; and finding none, he saith, I will return into my house whence I came out. 25. And when he cometh, he finds it swept and garnished. 26. Then goeth he, and taketh to him seven other spirits more wicked than himself; and they enter in and dwell there: and the last state of that man is worse than the first."

Here we see the evil spirit, after being forced to leave his victim, having to wander in "dry" places. As "water" is the symbol of mana, the "dry place" is the symbol of the lack of mana. The spirit, unable to steal mana was without rest. The word for "rest"[3] is also the word for "to steal," so the code tells us the spirit found no place where he could steal mana. But, he returns hopefully to his victim, and there finds him —pictured as a "house"—all swept and garnished. The key word here is "swept".[4] This has several meanings, one of which is "to plait; to twist." (Brushes were braided with feathers at the base by the kahunas and used as dusters.) The symbol of putting to use the shadowy cord reaching to the High Self is "to braid" and this braiding also suggests the existence of a cord. To sweep with a plaited or braided brush has a special meaning of "to scatter" and applied to particles of dust, these being hard to see and so like the thought-forms of prayers are "scattered" and so wasted. Here we have the coded information that when a spirit has been cast out, and when the victim contiues to fail to recognize his High Self and to begin asking it in prayer to take its rightful part in living the three-fold life, the "house" is left open and unguarded. The word, "garnished" repeats the idea of the "braided cord" because the kahuna people, in making ready for a guest, garnished their houses by braiding wreaths of decorative greenery and flowers to hang here and there and to place around the necks of guests. The word[5] for "garnished" has also the meaning of *providing a goodly supply of everything a guest might need.* This points to the victim, still filled with mana, and with no protection, so the evil spirit goes to find his evil friends, and they play the part of the guests, taking over again, but in greater numbers.

Mark gives us a valuable code word when he tells of the casting out of an unclean spirit obsessing a man in a synagogue. In 1:25, we read, "and Jesus rebuked him saying, Hold thy peace and come out of him." The code word here

3. *Maha.*
4. *Kahili.*
5. *Hoo-lakolakoia.*

is "rebuke,"[6] which also means "*to shine, or create light and heat,*" symbolizing the opening of the path of the man so that the "Light" or High Self could help in removing the evil spirit.

NOTE: In his sayings, as well as direct teaching, Jesus continually spoke of "my, our, or your Father which is in heaven." The root *au* for "I" or "self" appears in each word. These, in the language of the code are, "*ko'u* (my), *kakau,* (our), *oukau* (your), *Makua* (parent). *Lani* is "heaven". It is of importance that we keep in mind the code fact that it takes both the father and the mother to make the parent, and that, in the word for "heaven," *la-ni,* we have the root *la* for Light, as the symbol of the High Self which is made up of a male and female self, and the obscure root *ni* which is found as *ni-ni* in the word meaning "*to heal,*" or in the word *ni-ni-ni* meaning *to pour out, as a liquid:* the healing given by the High Self in answer to prayer is accomplished by the use of the mana which is usually supplied by the one who makes the Huna-type prayer for healing.

6. *Papa.*

CHAPTER 5

The Parables

It is impossible to follow a direct sequence in a study such as this in which we are watching for the code behind significant events in the life of the Master.

Our Lord lived, healed, taught, and the story, as we have it, must be taken in sections in order to see the inner teachings.

Two outstanding things which Jesus taught secretly, and stressed repeatedly in various ways, were THE NATURE OF PRAYER and THE CORRECT WAY TO MAKE A PRAYER. We will discuss these at length as we go along, for they are of the greatest importance.

We will also pause as we go along to see how the lack of understanding of the hidden meaning resulted in the formation of many false beliefs in the Christian religion of early days—many of which have been retained up to the present time.

THE PARABLE OF THE SOWER

With Matthew, 13:3, we begin to read the parable of the sower.

"Behold, a sower went forth to sow; 4. And when he sowed, some *seeds* fell by the wayside, and fowls came and devoured them up: 5. Some fell upon stony places, where they had not much earth: and forthwith they sprang up, because they had no deepness of earth: 6. And when the sun was up, they were scorched, and because they had no root, they withered away. 7. And some fell among thorns; and the thorns sprung up, and choked them; 8. But others fell into good ground, and brought forth fruit, some an hundred fold, some sixtyfold, some thirtyfold. 9. Who hath ears to hear, let him hear. 10. And the disciples came, and said unto him, Why speakest thou unto them in parables? 11. He answered and said unto them, Because it is given unto you to know the mysteries of the kingdom of heaven, but to them it is not given. For whosoever hath, to him shall be given, and he shall have more abundance: but whosoever hath not, from him shall be taken away even that which he hath. 13. Therefore speak I to them in parables: because they seeing see not; and hearing they hear not, neither do they understand.''

This is the most open reference imaginable to the fact that a MYSTERY or SECRET teaching lay behind his words. The ''mysteries of the kingdom of heaven'' were the mysteries of the High Self Father. And Jesus quotes the initiate, Isaiah, to give double strength to the fact that a secret teaching is being presented. We read: ''14. And in them fulfilled the prophesy of Esaias, which saith, By hearing ye shall hear, and shall not understand; and by seeing ye shall see, and shall not perceive: 15. For this people's heart is waxed gross, and their ears are dull of hearing, and their eyes have closed; lest at any time they should see with their eyes and hear with their ears, and should understand with their hearts, and should be converted and I should heal them. 16. But blessed are your eyes, for they see; and your ears, for they hear. 17. For verily I say unto you, That many prophets and righteous men have desired to see these things which ye see, and have not seen them; and to hear these things which ye hear, and have not heard them. Hear ye therefore the parable of the sower.''

THE OUTER EXPLANATION OF THE PARABLE then followed and I will quote it so that we can have before us the several related passages, after which we will go on to the inner teaching as revealed by the code.

"19. When any one heareth the word of the kingdom, and understandeth it not, then cometh the wicked one, and snatcheth away that which was sown in his heart. This is he that received seed by the wayside. 20. But he that received the seed into stony places, the same is he that heareth the word, and anon with joy receiveth it. 21. Yet hath he not root in himself, but dureth for a while: for when tribulation or persecution ariseth because of the word, by and by he is offended. 22. He also that received seed among the thorns is he that heareth the word; and the care of this world, and the deceitfulness of riches, choke the word, and he becometh unfruitful. 23. But he that received the seed into the good ground is he that heareth the word, and understandeth it; which also beareth fruit, and bringeth forth, some an hundredfold, some sixty, some thirty."

The Secret Or Inner Teaching

No other code word was given so much importance or so many meanings as "seed".[1] The several meanings make certain that we miss no part of the instructions which enable us to make a prayer that is effective and which will be rewarding in terms of answers. Let me list the meanings and show what each has to do with the making of a perfect prayer. (It is interesting to note that the kahunas of Polynesia spoke of a prayer as "Well made," or as "not well made, and so useless".)

1. *Likeness, resemblance, image of a thing.* This meaning instructs us to be sure to make the proper mental picture of what we wish to pray for—the proper thought form. The picture is NOT to be one such as embodied in a phrase like, "Help me to get a healthy stomach". That is the old and defective method. One must make a mental picture of the PERFECT stomach and digestion, and believe that the new condition has already been created by the father in the material of the shadowy body and that this is the "seed" which, if watered daily by sending a flow of mana along the

1. *Ano* or *anoano*, and with *hou, hou ano.*

shadowy cord to the Father, will eventually materialize and appear in the dense level of the physical world. Jesus said, "Ask believing that you have already received." This is an exertion of FAITH, but not blind faith—this is faith based on inner knowledge, and is of the kind "that moves mountains". Most prayers are imporperly made, are not kept growing by the daily sending of mana, and are allowed to wither and die because we grow impatient or give up hope. Jesus said, "Pray without ceasing", and now we see what he meant.

2. *A word or phrase.* This meaning tells us that when we speak or think in terms of words and phrases, we are making the thought form picture of what we want. But if we do not give sufficient thought ahead of time to what we wish to have come to pass for us, we may be asking for a White Elephant. One should take plenty of time to decide just what is wanted and how to word a prayer that will describe it with exact accuracy. The kahunas had a habit of repeating their prayer three times over to be sure they had made the picture just right as they renewed it and sent it daily with the watering mana to the High Self.

3. *To halo or consecrate; to set apart for a special purpose.* This is the process of setting aside or presenting to the High Self a certain amount of mana to be sent with the prayer.

4. *Fear.* This is the idea embodied in the phrase, "Fear of the Lord", and has the meaning of to be very careful to observe all the rules of living and of prayer making. Fear of change on the part of the low self may cancel a prayer.

5. *Now.* This is the meaning which tells us of the picturing of the outcome of the prayer as "now" or already given as the completed answer to prayer.

6. *To have a form or appearance* (and with *hou)* to be new, to *change* the form *or appearance* of a *person or thing.* Here we have the basic meaning of the changes which must be made by the High Self to create the answer to a prayer.

Jesus was talking in veiled language about the "seeds" or thought forms which one makes when constructing a prayer before sending it with a flow of vital force along the shadowy cord to the Superconscious or Father. (See how delightfully simple it is, once we know what to look for?)

We read that the sower scattered the seeds, and here we have more code words. The seeds that "fell by the wayside" and were devoured by the "birds of the air" were the prayer pictures which were never sent to the High Self because of the blocked path—this blocking caused by "spirits" (represented by the symbol of birds or fowl), who may influence a praying person to his detriment, and may also steal the mana he may try to send along the shadowy cord.

"Some fell on stony places, where there was not much earth: and forthwith they sprang up, because they had no deepness of earth: and when the sun was up, they were scorched, and because they were rootless, they withered away." Here we have the code in *withered*[2] which means "dried out" and is the symbol of lack of mana or water. The whole passage tells us of the badly made prayer, not well thought out to begin with, and not followed through steadfastly with daily sending of mana to "water" the prayer "seeds" and allow the Father to grow them into the ultimate answer to the prayer.

"Some fell among thorns,[3] and the thorns sprung up and choked them. . . ." The code meaning for "thorns" is: *to break; to shiver with fear or cold.* From the roots we get, light as the symbol of the High Self; *to call for a thing desired; to approach or draw near to someone or to some place; a bird.* Here we see that the prayer is broken (perhaps by obsession) in that the low self refuses to send the prayer because it "fears" the new conditions which are asked for by the middle self—who makes the prayer in the first place. This is why, when we start making over our lives and deciding what changes we want to get made with the help of prayer, we should take plenty of time and picture ourselves in the new place or new condition. In the process of such picturing one usually will get a strong feeling from the low self to tell one that it is not willing to let go of the OLD. Here we have the word FEAR at its best code meaning, and the word for thorn which has been given, has the alternate meaning of "to shiver as with fear or cold". If the low self fears the change to the NEW, it will block

2. *Maloo*: to dry out or wither.
3. *Kaka-lai-oa* .

the path. (Jesus wore a crown of thorns, and when on the cross prayed to the Father for help, and the prayer was blocked or *broken*. The help was not given.)

"But other fell into good ground, and brought forth fruit, some an hundred fold, some sixtyfold, some thirtyfold. Who hath ears to hear, let him hear." In this we have the prayers which are well made and which conform to all the rules. They are answered when the "growth" is completed, and the reward is great.

"For whosoever hath, to him shall be given, and he shall have more abundance: but whosoever hath not, from him shall be taken away even that which he hath." Here we have a passage which has for years puzzled those who have had only the outer teaching. It seems so unkind and so contrary to what we are led to expect from a God of love and mercy. But thanks to the code and our understanding of the inner meanings, we can see that the reference here is to the person who HATH—who HATH UNDERSTANDING OF THE HIDDEN WAY OF PRAYER and who is promised "abundance." The one who "hath not" just blunders along, and what little trace of understanding he may have had is soon lost in a tangle of false dogmas and "teachings" given by the self-appointed leaders who try from the pulpit to expound the true teachings.

If we had nothing else in the Gospels to instruct us, this great lesson on prayer would be almost enough. But the explanation is repeated in several ways, always using the code, to make sure that the "elect" would fully understand. Soon we will see what additions to the method are offered by the Master.

The OUTER EXPLANATION given by Jesus needs little comment. The "word" used here has the meaning of the combined outer and inner teachings. It is explained that some hear and understand but fall by the wayside in time, some follow the teachings for a little longer period before falling away, and the few hold the faith to the end. There is no code used here with the intention of instruction of the chosen pupils.

The quotation from Isaiah condemns the people of his day

"whose hearts had waxed gross" as unworthy of receiving the secret teachings. Jesus repeats this to point out the unworthiness of the masses to receive initiation.

THE SEED AS SYMBOL OF DEATH AND RESURRECTION

From early Egypt down through the Greek mysteries there had been a belief in a resurrection. The seed was the symbol of the same cycle of life followed by man. The seed was said to die when planted, as was the man in burial, but there followed a new life.

The kahunas, like the sages of India, believed that man reincarnated, and it is quite posssible that this was also a belief taught by Jesus in secret. To reincarnate and live in perhaps a dozen bodies to gain experience, seems to have been the rule in so far as the kahunas were concerned. Unlike the men of India, they did not believe in almost endless rounds of incarnation.

The first great secret had to do with the salvation which came when one realized, that he had a High Self Father and could pray in the proper manner and get help. The second and final salvation will be taken up later. In it one reaches the end of all incarnating and graduates a step up the evolutionary scale to become a High Self.

THE PARABLE OF THE MUSTARD SEED

The parable of the mustard seed is simply a variation of the one of the sower. The point here is that the mustard seed is so small that it is almost as nebulous as the mental picture of the prayer, but when it is grown into the answer, it is large and strong to the point of being almost a tree.

In a similar way, the very tiny thing which stands for the "seed" of the prayer, is likened to the leaven which the woman hid in three measures of meal, but which soon grew to leaven the whole. The growth from a mental picture to a materialized or earthly condition, situation or object, is a similar progression from the immaterial to the material. . . . In this case the "meal" that rises or increases in size represents the "seed" watered by mana and made to grow.

Reading farther in this chapter which is famous for its parables, (Matt. 13) we come, in verse 34, to the section in which Jesus explained the parable meanings as, "things which have been kept secret from the foundation of the world."

The actual explanation begins with verse 37 in which he says, "He that soweth the good seed is the Son of man." From the Huna lore we draw the inference that the lesser pair of selves, as the "Son of man" must sow the seeds, that is, make the prayer and use "good seeds" or carefully selected prayer goals.

Jesus continues, "The field is the world. . . ." In the code the word for *world*[4] means *light*, so we see here the double meaning in which the High Self becomes the "field" in which the good seed is planted. Continuing, ". . . the good seed are the children of the kindom. . . ." This repeats the fact that the seeds are to be planted with the High Self, for it is "the kingdom" in the inner symbology. The idea of "children" suggests growth to maturity, as growth of seeds to fruition. ". . . but the tares are the children of the wicked one." The poorly made prayer or the one in which a person prays for something harmful to others to come to pass, comes under the heading of the "tares." The High Self will have no part in bringing about a condition which hurts others or which may deprive someone of the use of his free will, even if he is a wayward son whose drunkenness may cause him to learn life's lessons the hard way.

Verse 39 is a rather obscure part of the explanation of the secret processes of Huna. It speaks of "the devil" as the one who planted the tares. In Huna there is no "devil," only darkness which is the opposite of light.[5] Only through ignorance will one plant tares for himself by praying for conditions which will hurt others if brought about. ". . . The harvest is the end of the world, and the reapers are the

---

4. *Ao:* world or light.
5. *Po:* darkness in contrast to *oo* or enlightenment.

angels." Here the "harvest"[6] is simply *to glean*, but the word "reapers"[7] in the code means *to reap* but *to be left destitute*, so we see that the man who makes the prayer with the wrong goals becomes the reaper or one who gets nothing at all from his prayers. The "angels" give a backward glance at the High Self who has seen to it that the hurtful prayer is rejected.

These Gospel passages, which on the face of them seem to tell of the "end of the world," when taken with passages describing the Parousia as something to happen very soon, or at least during the lifetime of the listeners, have caused much misunderstanding, with some Christian sects still basing their claim of correct information on the forlorn expectations which for almost 2,000 years have been unfulfilled.

Continuing our reading with verse 40, the writer repeats in slightly different words what he has just presented. However, in verse 42 another code word is inserted and we read, "there shall be wailing and gnashing of teeth." The outer meaning seems to be that human beings who are evil will be cast into the fires at the end of the world, but the code words[8] give us, *to wail, weep and cry with tears*—the tears being water and symbolizing mana and "to gnash the teeth or *to wring water out of something to dry it.* In both of these words we have the coded information that the "tares" or evil prayer pictures will have the water or mana taken from them so that the "seeds" will dry out and not grow.

Verse 43 gives a triumphant ending to the secret teachings, "Then shall the righteous[9] (meaning *good*, or *those without darkness*—the good seeds) shine forth as the sun in the kingdom of their Father." The good seeds will flourish as the answer to the prayer takes more and more material form. "Who hath ears to hear, let him hear." The last phrase indicates that what has been said above is part of the secret lore and is to be understood only by the initiates who have learned to hear the code words and know their secondary meanings.

In verse 45 we have another parable started. "Again, the kingdom of heaven is like unto a merchantman, seeking goodly pearls: Who, when he had found one pearl of great

6. *Oki* to harvest or reap.
7. *Oki-oki*: reapers; destitutes.
8. *Uwe* and *uwi*.
9. *Pono*.

price, went and sold all he had and bought it." In the preceding verse a man finds a treasure buried in a field and sells all in order to buy the field. There are no particular code words here, but as the kingdom is being described, we see that the "good seed" or prayer for something which is really good for the growth and well-being of the lesser man, is treasured highly by the High Self and all possible efforts are made to exchange the present unwanted conditions for the good and desirable conditions. Buying and selling, is, in the code,[10] to exchange one thing for another, or here, the bad old conditions for good new ones.

In many religions the problem of the good and the bad men has been dealt with in various ways. In Huna the bad men appear to have been looked upon as those still darkened and low in the evolutionary scale. They are not condemned to a hell, but are thought to be under the loving care of their own High Selves who bear with them with endless patience and help in every possible way to guide them into the light.

Only a few religions have presented the belief that part of humanity is of the devil and can never be saved. In the Gospels the "elect" and the "chosen" are now mentioned, and the outer circle teaching has seemed to be that only these favored ones can be saved, but that the rest are naturally evil and are not worth saving, the final Judgment being looked upon as the time when the tares will be separated from the good grain and burned in the everlasting fire by an impatient God.

Christianity, set against the Jewish background, inherited to some extent in its outer doctrines the vengeful God of the prophets. This unloving and impatient attitude appears in the parable of the rich man who forgave the money debts of a man who came before him unable to pay. The same man then went to find one who owed him a small amount and showed him no mercy, taking him by the throat to force payment. When the rich and generous man, standing in the place of God in the parable, was told of the complete selfishness of the man he had so helped, he angrily revoked the earlier forgiveness and demanded the payment of the entire debt.

10. *Kuai.*

(Matt. 18:34-35) "And his lord was wroth, and delivered him to the tormentors until he should pay all that was due unto him."

THE PARABLE OF THE PRODIGAL SON

Luke gives us some parables not mentioned by Matthew, Mark or John. The Parable of the Prodigal son is one of these, and contains little or no coded meaning. The outer teaching gives us the fact that the Father is ever loving and forgiving and anxious to have his wayward sons and daughters return to him, reformed and willing to try to do better. The path must be opened and we must begin to invite the THIRD ELEMENT OF THE HUMAN TRINITY, the Father, to take his part in our lives. He will do this only when recognized and asked to do so. He must be asked in prayer.

The Prodigal Son lost contact, or never had it, with his Father, and, like most men, tried to live his life without Help or Guidance. He suffered greatly, but with the Father to help him, found comfort and prosperity.

There were other parables, but for our study, they are not too important. What is important is the making of an effective prayer, so let us go on to consider the secret method which enables us to accumulate extra mana and have it ready to send with the thought forms of the prayer to the High Self.

THE HA RITE

The method of accumulating extra mana is simple. The word for *breath* or *to breathe*[1] codes the hidden method and has also the meaning of *four*, or *forty*. It was taken for granted that this would be taught to the elect at the same time that they were taught about the mana, the shadowy cord that leads to the High Self, and the thought forms of the prayer.
NOTE: For ease of handling I will give the code words in the text as I go along.

Ha, for *four*, also means *to breathe strongly*, and this gives us the method of accumulating extra mana. It also means, *a trough or tube for running water*, symbolizing the sending of the flow of mana to the High Self.

KAU-NA, the alternate word for *four*, gives us the root, *kau*, and this has great value in the code because of its many meanings, one of which is, *to place something in a designated place*, and in which we see the idea of placing the mana and thought-form "seeds" of the prayer in the keeping of, or place of, the High Self. The meaning of *to set before one, as food*, points to the offering of mana to the High Self. Another meaning is, *to fall upon; to embrace affectionately*, in which we have the code of love shown the lesser man by the High Self. The 17th meaning listed in the dictionary is, *to rehearse in the hearing of another that he may learn*, this giving us the idea of repeating the prayer often and without changing it. The 22nd meaning is, *to place and then to rest*, which describes the action taken in making the prayer, the mana and thought-form picture being "placed" with the High Self, and the completed action then stopped or rested.

The importance of accumulating mana was shown by the kahunas in their word, *hoo-mana*, which means *to worship*, and which also means *to make mana*. The High Self is said to lack mana because it has no physical body, and to depend on the low self for what it needs in its ordinary activities when away from the lower man. When we are asleep it is supposed to touch us and take a little mana, but for the heavy charges needed to work in the materials of the dense or physical world, much mana is needed.

The Secret Of Sacrifice

The secret of making a sacrifice is that mana must be accumulated and then sent to the High Self along the shadowy cord. When we are happy and contented we can "worship" the Father by accumulating mana and sending it as a gift which the High Self can use as it sees fit.

The outer teachings about the making of a sacrifice were wrong and barbaric. The blood was supposed to contain the very life of the animal, and so blood was sprinkled over altars and in purification rites. In the churches we sing about being "saved by the blood of the lamb", and this "blood" is supposed to purify and so to give salvation. It can do nothing of the sort. The rite of sacrifice was probably encouraged by an ignorant priesthood, the priests sprinkling the altars with the blood, and later eating the meat of the sacrificial creature. The only possible sacrifice we can make that is acceptable to the High Self is MANA.

THE ACCUMULATION OF MANA

One can think an order to the low self to begin to accumulate mana, and then demand its attention by taking away its automatic job of breathing for us and causing the breath to come more deeply and regularly for four breaths, then pausing a few seconds and repeating the process. The four-breath rhythm is easy to learn to fall into, and the meaning of *forty* (for *ha*) gives us about the limit of the breaths needed for the accumulation.

One can stand, sit, be walking or at work. Usually one quiets down and gets ready for the making of one's prayer or for the daily or hourly repetition of a prayer already made but which is repeated word for word to strengthen the thought form prayer picture and to send more mana to enable the High Self to continue growing the seeds into the matured answer to the prayer.

In the Old Testament story of the creation of Adam and Eve, the "life" was breathed into the clay image of Adam. This symbolizes the mana as the life force. The Egyptians knew the life force of breath. The Greeks gave us the word "spirit", which comes from their word for "breath", as the highest of the divine beings. We read of "the Spirit of God", but this is an outer meaning for a great inner truth—the truth of "the breath of life". When Jesus says, "I am the life", he codes for us the meaning of mana, and that alone. He was not that "life". He taught the great truths about the "life" or mana.

The makers of the code, back in the earliest days of Egypt, were very careful to preserve the secret meanings. Not only did they give us the number FOUR as a code symbol of great importance, but they described the details of the prayer making art in the numbers one, two and three. These code many things for us. But, after four, the numbering coded nothing at all. Let us examine the numbers and their meanings.

Ka-hi: "one". This word, as the maker of the dictionary explains, was often used in place of one pronounced at times in almost the same way, *ka-he*, both have the meaning of "*to cut longitudinally*," (split open) which was, with the Huna people, "to circumcise." Behind this strange custom of circumcision, which has spread around half the world and which even the Australian Arunta people practiced, lies the secret meaning of sacrifice—the sacrifice of a part of the creative or life force. The male sex organ was symbolic of this creative force, and with many ancient peoples the circumcision rite was one of great importance. It was accompanied by special acts and, with some tribes was part of the initiation of a boy into the estate of manhood.

It is most interesting to find that there was no definite reason given in the Bible where, in Genesis 17:10–27, God was said to have spoken to Abram, ordering him to establish a new covenant between his people and their God. In this covenant all males were to be circumcised, but no reason was given for the command. One suspects the re-establishment of an older custom, or the borrowing of one from some other religion. The Huna system would seem to be the most likely source as it was evidently older, and as it gave its secret word code a reason for the practice.

This reason is to be seen in the code words and their roots. *Oki* is *to cut*, and *omaka* is the *foreskin*. That gives the outer meaning. The code meaning comes from the secondary meanings of the words or roots. To cut is also *kahi*, meaning (1) *The Number One*, (2) *A place*; and (3) the pronoun, *one*. As *cut*-it has the meaning of *opening*, and in the alternate word, *kahe* the secondary meaning is *a flow of blood*. The thing to be opened by cutting, and with the accompanying flow of blood, is the *omaka* or foreskin, but this word also means, *the fountainhead of a stream of water* (water symbolized mana), and in this we have the secret. The covenant was one established in Huna with the godlike High Self, and the creative force or mana was to be sent as a gift or sacrifice. The cutting, foreskin and blood flow stand as outer symbols for a pact or pledge to supply the High Self with the mana it needs to perform its part of the work of living—living as part of the three-self man. Perhaps no better example can be found of the misunderstanding of a Huna code teaching, and its blind use in outer form, than that of circumcision. We see clearly that the Ha Rite of prayer, starting with the count of "one" calls for the accumulation and sending of mana to the High Self, certainly not for the actual cutting of the foreskin. (The women kahunas were on a par with the men, and sent mana to the High Selves in the usual way, and they, naturally, were not circumcised.)

That the rite was very ancient, is shown by the traditional use of a flint knife for circumcision. In Egypt the religious aspect of the rite was very clearly outlined in the fact that Horus, son of Osiris and Isis, died and was resurrected as a part of the Mystery of Amenta, and was shown then in his statues and paintings as circumcised. The Mohammedans borrowed the rite from the Israelites and used it, but in India and China, if practiced, circumcision had no religious significance. Only in Yoga is there a trace of the belief that the life force is connected in some way with the male sex organs, for "serpent force," or *prana,* was supposed to originate in the genitals, rise along the spine and pass out through the top of the head during the performance of elaborate breathing exercises which were accompanied by mental visualizations. The Yoga practitioners believed that the *prana* (mana) they accumulated was drawn from the air. The kahunas seem only to have known that the heavier breathing made the accumulation of extra mana possible. In modern times we would say that the extra oxygen taken in was used to burn blood sugar already circulating in the blood stream, and thus make of it the vital force. It is evident that in Yoga there was once a knowledge of the Ha Rite, but that as time passed, the reason for accumulating mana was lost. In "arousing the serpent force" it came to be sent from the body through the "Door of Brahm" or top of the head, but after leaving the body its destination became Supreme God, not the Father or High Self.

Getting back to the code word, *ka-hi* once more, we find in the root, *hi,* the secondary meaning of (1) *to flow away,* and (2) *to be weak.* This would tell us little if we did not already know that it was the mana which flowed like its symbol, water, and the flow was directed at the time of making the Ha Rite prayer to the High Self, which is "weak" if not supplied with mana. Those initiated into Huna learn that this mana-sending "covenant" between the lower pair of selves and the High Self is to be observed daily, without fail, and its observation marks the initiate as one above the lower ranks.

The code also places in *kahi*, for *one*, two other significances for the initiate. The three-self man becomes "one" when the contact with the High Self is made in performing the Ha Rite. The meaning of *a place* is better understood if we look for the "place" to which the flow of mana is directed—the place of the High Self.

E-lua or *A-lua* is *two*. The root *alu* also means *weak*, and so we have a repetition of one code meaning in the number "one" (it was a common practice in presenting the code to use more than one word to repeat the inner meaning lest it be overlooked). The same root, *alu*, means to *combine; to aid or give assistance; and to adhere*. These meanings point to the combining of the three selves in the prayer work.

The root, *e* in *elua*, the alternate word for *two*, has the meaning of, (1) *to call or invite attention*, which codes the low self making contact with the High Self; (2) *something strange or new*, and this description fits the High Self, especially when the root, *e*, is doubled to make *ee*, which means *something out of sight*.

An odd but important significance is to be found in the meaning of *alu*, to break or crumble to pieces. This codes the Huna belief that the future is automatically made for us by the High Self out of the shadowy substance, in a "pattern world" on its level. It is made to match our plans and hopes and even fears. When we decide to ask in prayer for quite a different future, the High Self must break up the patterns already formed and begin to build them again to fit the prayer.

The roots *lua* and *lu* give us *seeds* and *to scatter seeds* as in sowing them. The belief here is that when we pray for something, we must make a mental picture of the desired thing or condition, and that this picture is composed of tiny thought-forms or ideas impressed on microscopic bits of the shadowy substance by the low self. These clusters of thought-forms are the "seeds" which must be sent floating with a flow of mana to the High Self, and if accepted, are then symbolically watered with mana and made to begin to grow into the thing which will be the "answer" to the prayer. *KO-LU* is *three*. Again we have a repeated root carried from the preceding number, *lu*, for *scattering seeds*. But in the root *ko* we have the sign of the possessive case which tells us in code that in making the prayer we must exert faith and believe that what we have asked has been built already in the pattern world by the High Self. We are reminded of the words of Jesus, ". . . believe that ye receive them, and ye shall receive them."

The root *ko* also means *to accomplish; to fulfill; to bring to pass*, and this tells us the part played by the High Self in the answering of prayer. There is also the meaning of, *to create; to beget; to obtain what one has sought after*. The High Self creates the patterns of the changed future for the man, and gradually brings about the new conditions.

In Hawaii when the missionaries arrived, the kahunas marveled that they made their prayers with no careful preparation ahead of time, and, especially, without the slow and deeper breathing to accumulate mana to send with the prayer when it was put into words.

They shook their heads and said, "These people are without breath, and their prayers are without mana." Thereafter the white people became known as "the breathless ones", or *ha-ole*, which means, *without breathing*.

The kahunas of the pre-missionary days would, at certain times of the year, gather the people around their simple temples and all would spend time deciding just what blessing for the land they would pray for. They breathed to create mana, and the officiating priest went through the ritual motions, old as Egypt, of gathering the shadowy threads from the people and braiding them into a strong cord that would symbolize the cord reaching to the Great Company of High Selves. Then he entered a special grass house, sacred to this use, and intoned the prayer three times. If all went well, he came out after a pause and announced that the prayer had been well made and would be effective.

The braided cord is symbolized in Japan by the strands of rope, a foot through in the center and one strand thick at the ends. These are suspended between two posts before the temples and signify, not the braiding of the cords as in Hawaii, but the power to be had in prayer when many people join together. The inner truth was lost in most places, but the symbols in one form or another were retained.

The Gospels are filled with words which when translated back into the code language, are found to contain the root *ha*. The secret was well kept, as befitted the protection of one of the most vital points in the teachings.

THE OUTER TEACHING ABOUT PRAYER

When the Lord (which is *ha-ku* in the code, the roots meaning *heavy breathing, and to raise up*, symbol of lifting mana to the High Self, and *to be right, fitting and proper*, as a well thought out and executed prayer should be,) was asked about prayer, of which he was a master initiate, he gave what we have come to call the "Lord's Prayer", but it was only the outer form. But the outer form was good in its way, and it coded some secrets of the prayers that got answered.

"Hallowed be thy name", gives us for "hallow", *ho-ano*, with the meaning of *to make or supply*, plus *to stretch out to touch*, plus *to carry or transfer* (as the seed and mana sent to the High Self); then the word for "seed" which we have explored and found packed with special meanings. So, we "hallow" by making the proper secret prayer.

The prayer was to be addressed to "Our Father", not to God or Jehovah, for prayer can only go to the place which is reached by the shadowy cord. ALL PRAYER GOES TO THE FATHER OR HIGH SELF, no matter to whom we think to direct it.

"Thy kingdom come" reminds us of the realm of the High Self, for this is the "kingdom" with which the inner teaching deals at all times. The "come" covers the first great salvation, that of learning that there IS a High Self, and making contact with it so that we can have all three selves working as a team and can have the great help and the wonderful guidance of the Father. "Thy will be done" indicated one's willingness to let the High Self decide what is best for us, and also points to the bringing down into the physical the answer to prayer which has been constructed in the realm of the High Self by an act of its will and the use of the "seed" and the "water-mana" sent to it.

"Give us . . ." is used frequently, and in the code it is *ha-awi*, in which we see the *ha* root for breath, and so are warned that this is an important part in the act of prayer if we are to expect an answer.

To "forgive others that we may be forgiven", has no particular code significance, nor has "Lead us not into temptation, but deliver us from evil."

The code word for prayer is *pu-le*, and means *to worship, to pray, or supplicate*. However, from the roots, *pu* and *le*, which have several separate meanings, we can gather the true secret of prayer. In addition to *call*, as to the High Self, we have *to hold water in the mouth while trying at the same time to talk*, and *to make something fly upward*. This symbolizes the mana which goes with the words or thought forms of the prayer to the High Self. (The kahunas, in their chants spoke of the *pule·o'o* or prayer which had *ripened or fully matured* and was a "prayer of power". This was the well made prayer after it had been accepted by the Father and after it had been made into the answer and returned to the one making the prayer.)

Jesus referred several times in his discourses to "those of little faith". The code word for no faith is *pau-lele*, which literally means, *to stop flying upward*, there we have the picturesque symbol of stopping the process of making a prayer in the proper fashion and then sending it "flying upward". We gather that if we have no confidence in the fact that there is a Father to hear us, we cannot pray well, and that is the secret of "lack of faith". Jesus said that if we had only as much faith as a "grain of mustard seed" our prayer could still move mountains. The mustard seed, being the "smallest of seeds", symbolizes the thought forms, and it is taken for granted that one knows that they must be sent on a "flow of mana-water" along the shadowy cord to the High Self.

"Knock and it shall be opened unto you," gives us the inner teaching in the word for "open", which is *ha-mana*, with the meaning from the roots of *to accumulate mana*, and *to make it accompany something*, in this case the thought forms of the prayer.

Jesus said, ". . . strait is the gate, and narrow is the way, which leadeth to life, and few there be that find it." Here we have the code word "way" (*la*) and the meaning of *a path*, with the code significance of the shadowy cord leading to the High Self, and, of course this presupposes a knowledge of the entire teaching concerning the Father and prayer.

Another bit from the words of the Master reads, "But Jesus said unto him, follow me, let the dead bury their dead." The word "follow" is the code word here. If we are to learn how to follow the Lord, we must know its secret meaning, which is (*ha-hai*), *to breathe hard*, to collect mana, and *to speak*, also *to break off doing evil things*. One root of the word suggests the whole prayer philosophy, and the other the wording of a prayer after turning over a new leaf in one's conduct and becoming hurt-less. The root *hai*, also has the meaning of *a sacrifice*, and indicates the necessity of offering mana to the Father.

We have "faith" mentioned in many cases of healing. Jesus said to the woman who touched the hem of his garment, "Thy Faith has made these whole." In the case of the two blind men whose eyes he touched after they had asserted that they knew he could heal them, he said, "According to your faith be it unto you." The word for "faith" is *mana-oio*, and the roots give us the secret of why faith helps to bring healing. We have, *Mana* plus *the real truth*, and in the root *to project, extend*, which repeats the teaching that the mana must be "projected" to the High Self to enable it to do the healing.

In John, 14:10–12, we have the coded statement which has been so misunderstood that it has become tangled with the idea that Jesus was God, and that his followers should be able to perform even greater miracles than he. We read,

"Believest thou not that I am in the Father, and the Father in me? The words that I speak unto you I speak not of myself: but the Father that dwelleth in me, he doeth the works. 11. Believe me that I am in the Father, and the Father in me: or else believe me for the very works' sake. 12. Verily, verily, I say unto you, He that believeth on me, the works that I do shall he do also; and greater works than these shall he do; because I go to my Father."

"Within" is our first code word, (*ma-loko*). It means *within* and from the root *loko* also means *a small body of water such as a pond*, calling the attention of an initiate reader to the involvement of mana in doing the works or having them done by the Father. Mana suggests the entire prayer rite.

The word "works" is *ha-na*, giving a very inclusive general meaning of *any kind of work or accomplishment or performance*. From the first root we have our now familiar pointer to the whole of the prayer rite involving breath, mana, etc.

It is not enough that one believe in the outer teachings of Jesus, one must also know the inner teachings in order to understand these passages and to perform the "works" with the help of the Father, who is within only in the sense that he is in contact with us through the mechanism of the shadowy cord. "Faith without works" is not enough. Mana and thought forms and the cooperation of the Father are necessary to complete the action.

Scattered all through the Gospels we find the coded instructions for the making of the correct prayer, but we have now taken up a sufficient number of incidents to serve our purpose, which is to show that the code was there and that the writers of the Gospels had used it to reveal to those who were of the elect, but conceal the inner truths from the outsiders.

Before moving on to the crucifixion, it may be well to say once more that it is evident from the accounts that Jesus was giving us a living example of what to do in living the progressive and hurtless life, and what not to do.

From the very nature of the inner teachings, we can see that the order of events given in the Gospels is in need of a slight reordering. Events and sayings were sometimes put into the story of the life of Jesus in a way that we can only correct when we have a knowledge of the inner truths. The Transfiguration, as we shall see, should come after the death and resurrection of the Master. And there are other matters which we will discuss which will demand that we go back through the scattered passages and sayings to pick up the special teachings and present them as a unit.

CHAPTER 6

The Mystery Of The Cross
And The Crucifixion

There are two distinct stories given in the Four Gospels which cover the life and ministry of Jesus. The first story tells of the expectation of Jesus that the "Last Day" was near and would come even during the lifetime of those who heard him tell of the opening of the heavens and the setting of the stage for the Last Judgment—with himself seated on the right hand of God-the-Father to act as judge.

In this version of the story, the coming of the "kingdom of Heaven" is a material event, not a spiritual accomplishment. The followers of Jesus were encouraged to expect the advent of the Messiah, but without having him conquer with armies and take over the earth as it then stood. The heavens would open and there would be no need for armies or worldly leadership—in fact, no time for such things. The end of the world would have come with divine intervention and the wicked would be separated from the good and destroyed in the fires of hell. The loving Father of the second version of the story was not to be there to search for the lost sheep and bring it into the fold.

In the second version of the story, Jesus expected only a spiritual kingdom of heaven to be gained, and then only by a few—the "elect" or "chosen." He expected to be made perfect, himself, after completing his ministry, and to be allowed to enter the kingdom. He failed the test at the end of the first life—the crucifixion marking the failure. He was resurrected and in the new life succeeded in gaining the necessary perfection and in being "transfigured"—symbolically entering the "kingdom."

In the first materialistic version of the story, Jesus confidently expects the Great Day to arrive. When it is delayed, he sends the "Seventy" to preach the Gospel far and wide in Israel, but even then nothing happens. At this point he changes his belief that the end is at hand, and goes a step farther in fitting himself into the picture of the "Righteous Servant" of Isaiah. He tells his Disciples that he will suffer the final and utter degradation, even being crucified, but rising from the dead after three days—after which his prediction breaks off abruptly with nothing said of the Last Day. (In this section, Matt. 20:18–19, Jesus says that he will "be delivered to the Gentiles to mock, and to scourge and to crucify him: and the third day he shall rise again.")

In John we are told hat Jesus knew all that was to happen to him, but no definite prediction was made as in Matthew. Again, nothing is said of the arrival of the Last Day and the Judgment.

In much the same way, we have the story made to fall into three teachings, the outer, the inner and the inner-final. Or, we could call these divisions, the outer salvation, the second salvation and the third and final salvation.

The mixing of the various versions and elements resulted in a tangle that even the code does not completely resolve. For instance, it is still not at all clear just why the command should be placed in the story as it was when Jesus is made to say, ". . . take up thy cross daily, and follow me." At that point in his life he had not yet predicted his own death on the cross.

In beginning our study of the crucifixion through the code, our first problem is to try to decide just why Jesus died on the cross, and whether or not his death had anything to do with the saving of mankind from the Adamic curse, as claimed by Paul.

In the Old Testament account, Satan, as the evil serpent, worked through Eve to tempt Adam to disobey the command of the Lord to stay away from the Tree of Life located in the garden.

The code symbology tells us that what happened in both legends was that evil spirits came to exert an undue influence on living men. They were the "devils" who had to be cast out by Jesus and the Disciples. And, as we shall soon see, they were the cause of the failure of Jesus to pass his first tests and enter the "kingdom of heaven," this failure resulting in the crucifixion, although in a later incarnation the "transfiguration" marked his successful passage into the next higher level of being. In the matter of evil spirit influence, it was basic Huna belief that no evil spirit could influence or live with or partly obsess a living person unless that person already had a taint of similar evil in him.

Adam and Eve, having been slightly evil, allowed themselves to be tempted to disobey God's commands, and as a result they were driven from the Garden of Eden and they, with all their descendants were made to suffer physical death. In addition, they were made to earn their bread by the sweat of their brows and to be plagued by tares and thorns in their crops.

The idea that Jesus was sacrificed by God to save humanity from the curse of Adam could have offered only salvation from the necessity of dying, and so symbolize some form of "eternal life"—a form which all agreed must be spiritual life in heaven, not in bodies made everlasting on earth. By the time Christianity began to take form, the sin of Adam had become one of disobedience. As disobedience is a human failing, it was not counted a major or Adamic sin in Genesis, for right upon the heels of the story of Adam and his children, follows the story of a drastic punishment for sin by the sending of the Flood.

Ten generations after Noah came Abram and the covenant of circumcision, which in the code is a pledge not to neglect to send mana to the High Self. To neglect to do so would be a sin, but not one which could be atoned for on a world scale by the death of Jesus. Abram became Abraham and would have sacrificed his own son as the necessary offering to Jehovah, but at the last moment was given something else just as satisfactory—and in terms of the code, this was mana to offer—a part of his very own life force.

Not much was developed from the early traditions and the early Hebrews had no rite in which they sought forgiveness for the taint of sin left upon them because they had descended from Adam. They made a large annual sacrifice and asked forgiveness for the current sins of the entire tribe, but not, it is to be supposed, for the Adamic sin.

The idea of heaping the sins of the people on a scapegoat and driving it into the wilderness came later. In Leviticus 16:18-22, we have the account of what Jehovah commanded Moses to instruct Aaron to do as a special rite to gain forgiveness for the sins of the people and himself, as High Priest. The blood of a bullock and of one of a pair of kid goats was to be sprinkled seven times upon the mercy seat of the Ark of the Covenant, and the second kid served as the scapegoat. In this recital there is no mention made of Adamic sin, and we may conclude that for them any such basic sin as that was cancelled out by the convenants which had been established earlier by Noah and Abraham.

When we inquire what the attitude of Jesus was concerning the necessity for a blood sacrifice to win forgiveness for sin, we find in the Gospels that he was entirely against the ancient beliefs concerning such sacrifice. He took it upon himself to forgive the sins of those whom he healed, or, without a show of authority simply stated, "Thy sins be forgiven thee." In Luke 6:37 we find him saying: "Forgive that ye shall be forgiven." This indicated the discarding of all the old Jewish rites of sacrifice. He said openly that he was giving a new teaching to replace all the old ones, and this command was, "Love ye one another." His chief quarrel with the orthodox Jews centered on his rejection of the old, bloody and savage sacrificial system and the ignoring of the equally savage Jehovah.

The belief that Isaiah had prophesied a "righteous servant," who would have to be killed and offered in the Jewish fashion as a blood sacrifice to Jehovah for the redemption of the sins of all the world, is in no way justified by the prophecies themselves when examined in the light of the code.

Let us take up the matter of the command of Jesus to take up one's cross daily, which had been mentioned as one of the prime objections to accepting the dogma of salvation through crucifixion. This command or admonition to the willing followers simply cannot be interpreted logically as a reference to the cross upon which Jesus was later to be crucified. We cannot escape the conclusion that behind the word "cross" is a hidden and a very different meaning.

Let us ask just what it was in terms of the code that was to be "taken up" each day as a preliminary to following Jesus. In the code we have the word *kea* used most often for "cross." In addition to having the meaning of two crossed timbers such as make the cross of the crucifixion, there is also meant the older form of X form of cross, we also know that it stood as the sign that something was taboo. A wooden X cross standing on the path leading to a Polynesian temple warned against any approach. In ancient magic an X mark was used to prevent the approach of any evil being or influence, and in later Christianity the same custom survived, with the other type of cross put to use. In the games of children we have "King's X" used to stop the action of an opponent player. Amulets which were worn around the neck or on the person for protection from evil forces, usually had an X ingredient in their designs. In the language of the code we have the main meaning *of kea,* for "cross," *to obstruct,* and this obstruction is usually one of movement along a path. As the "path" is the symbol of the shadowy cord running from the lesser man to the High Self, we must inquire what it is that moves over this "path" which is obstructed. There is but one answer: a flow of mana. The flow is intended to carry the thought-form prayer picture to the High Self. In any case, the basic idea is that of something that prevents normal interchange between the lesser man and his High Self. Huna symbolizes this type of obstruction also as "a stumbling block in the path." Another symbol is a "knot" in the shadowy cord leading to the High Self, the knot stopping the mana flow.

A second code word for cross is *a-mana,* and in this case the Y cross is usually indicated, the example being the *Y branching of the two tree limbs.* This is the symbol of division. The fingers of the hand may be held in a V to denote the same thing, and the secret meaning of this kind of division is the dividing of the mana between the lesser man and the High Self. The root *mana* in the word also tells us *what is being divided*, and the root *ama* means *to feed* or *to satisfy with food* as in offering made to the gods. "Food" symbolizes mana as a sacrificial offering made to the High Self.

The answer to the question of what is to be taken up as a cross, is unquestionably mana. And, as the "cross" is to be taken up or lifted up daily, we have the Ha Rite and the sending of mana to the High Self.

This meaning is reinforced in the code word for "take up," which is *kaikai*, the secondary meaning of which is *to lift up on the hands and carry something along*, this points to the *"lifting up"* of the mana along the shadowy cord. The root, *kai* means *sea water*, and as water symbolizes mana, we have the meaning repeated obliquely.

"To follow" was a very adroit way of repeating the meanings already given. *Ha-hai* means, *to follow*, and in the *ha* root we have the symbol of the entire Ha Rite of prayer. The second root *hai* means *sacrifice* acceptable to the High Self—that of mana. (In calling his Disciples, Jesus said, "come and follow me." Here the meaning is the same.)

Thus, the code shows that the entire phrase, ". . . take up thy cross daily and follow," can be paraphrased in the secret admonition "to keep the path to the High Self open and send along it daily the gift of mana."

Luke adds to this admonition a mysterious command, "to deny" oneself, and the only thing which could be denied or given up in this case is part of one's mana, as we see in *hoo-le-mana*, which is the word for *deny* and which, in the root *le*, gives us *something made to fly* upward, the "something" being specified in the following root, *mana*. Again, we see stressed the necessity of opening the path and sending the mana to the High Self.

The Church saw only the outer meaning and set about deciding what a man should "deny" himself. Sex gratification was placed at the top of the list, and following that came practically everything which a man could possibly do without. An accompanying dogma for "follow Me" drove all the faithful to preach the Gospel, and to become missionaries, hermits and zealots. Those who resisted "the call" and continued to live normal lives with their families were usually tinged with a deep sense of guilt because they had not "answered the call."

Continuing, in verse 24, Luke's account reads, "For whosoever will save his life shall lose it: but whosoever will lose it for my sake, the same shall save it." We know that mana is the life force, and here we find Jesus speaking as the High Self. The statement, opened by the use of the code symbology, tells us that when we give part of our life force to the High Self, and in turn the High Self sends back a return flow to bless and cleanse and help the lesser man, "life" is regained in full and normal form.

Matthew and Mark (20:28 and 11:45) give a word-for-word series of passages which seem to show that Jesus, by his own words, described himself as a saviour. We read, "Even as the Son of man came not to be ministered unto, but to minister, and to give his life a ransom for the many."

If in this saying, Jesus meant that he would save the world by his death, nothing in his teaching could have been more important. But neither Luke nor John thought the passage of sufficient importance to record it. However, the code gives the inner meaning.

The word for "minister" in the code is *lawe-lawe*, which means to *serve another*, but the root word, *lawe* holds the key to the inner meaning of such service. It is *to transfer from one place to another* and one may well ask what it was that could be so transferred as an act of service, if not mana sent to the High Self.

We have already seen that mana is the life force—the very life of man—and so need not pause to inspect *ola*, (of the light) for "life." We go on to the word "give" as in "give his life." It is *ha-awi*, in which the root, *ha*, is our familiar symbol of gathering a surcharge of mana while breathing heavily and sending it as a gift to the High Self, (the root *awi*, we are told in the dictionary, was not found, but it may well have been *awe*, which has the meaning of a *thread or strand*, which would at once give us the shadowy thread along which the mana gift flows to the High Self).

The last key word is "ransom," and in the Hawaiian translation of the Gospels from English, the early missionaries and their helpers must have been uncertain just which of two words should be used, for in Matthew they used *lawe-lawe* which we have just seen to mean *transfer from one place to another*, and in Mark they used *hoo-kau-waia*, which the root *kau* has, as one of its many meanings, that of *placing something in a designated high place or setting food before someone*. The mana is sent to the "high place" symbolizing always the High Self, and it is often spoken of as "food" in the Huna lore where sending mana was called "feeding the god." The root *wa* means *the space between two things*, indicating the separation by space of the lesser man and the Father—the space across which the mana flows along the shadowy cord. Here there is also a neat play on words to give the code further meaning in the passages. The passive form of the full word is made by adding *ia* at the end, and so we have the root *wai* in *waia*, and once again, mana as symbolized by water.

In the outer teachings of the Gospels the words "ransom" and "redeem" have long since become confused. Jesus is said to have been sacrificed by God in the Crucifixion as a "ransom" paid to "redeem" all those who could not possibly have escaped Hell's fires because they still were under the curse of the Fall of Adam and Eve.

We have just seen that the coded inner teaching concerning a "ransom" dealt only with the sacrifice or gift of mana made to the Father High Self so that the properly made prayer could be duly answered.

The answer to the prayer was "redemption," or *hoola*, to restore light or life (*ho* or *hoo* can be used as the causative *to make* or *to bring about*). *La* is light and *ola*, *life*. Healing and all of the help in living given by the Father comes under the heading of "restore life" or "redeem." Jesus taught the sacrifice of mana as the "ransom" and the High Self as the "redeemer."

Taking up the events which led to the crucifixion, we need to keep watch for the coded units which tell us why Jesus failed in his initiation and died on the cross at the end of the great First Act of the story. We must ask ourselves what it was that prevented Jesus from passing the initiatory tests, and if we conclude that it was some form of "sin," we must ask what this sin could have been.

To begin with, we are told that Jesus was "betrayed," and here we have the code word, *hoo-ku-maka-ia*, which is, literally, to have *an eye set on one*, and equated with "the evil eye" of black magic, and the placing of a curse on one. The root, *kuma*, indicates that one is made *to stand with a company of others*, and as curses are placed by the sending of evil spirits to mislead or injure the one cursed, we have here the intimation that Jesus became the victim of the very "devils" whom he had so often cast out of others. One must watch to see what had happened that laid him open to this spirit invasion or interference. In Huna we learn that we attract evil spirits to us only in and to the degree of our own evil.

Helpless in the hands of his enemies, he was tried, scourged, crowned with thorns and made to carry a cross which was so heavy that it was beyond his strength and he could not. He fell, and another man had to be pressed into service. This inability to "take up" his cross gives us the symbol of inability to remove the blocking of his path.

Thorns are one of the symbols of blockings, and compare with snare and tare and net. The compelling influence of evil spirits is a greater disaster than suffering from a misconception or a fixation. To be caught in a net, to be snared, or to be entangled in a thorny bramble hedge, all symbolize spirit interference.

We have already considered the code words for "cross" and know it to be the major symbol of the blocked path. *Kau-la* is the code word for *the scourging*, this being done with a whip made up of several heavy cords. The word means *a stripe* and we recall the prophecies of Isaiah, in which the righteous servant was made to suffer with "stripes." The root *kau* means *to hang up; to crucify*; also *to light down on one, as a bird*, and here we have the evil spirits symbolized by birds. There is still another meaning of the root which may well apply here, it being, *to come upon one unexpectedly*, and from this we may guess

that the evil spirits which gained control of
his path had taken him completely by surpɪ
him off guard. The root *la* is the familiar syn
it tells us that the High Self was involved in
code meaning. The meaning of the full wor
and so we find that we are being told once ɪ
cord to the High Self had been blocked and
cause of the trouble.

The word for "cup" as in the "cup of bitterness" which was
to be drained by Jesus, we have the code word *pai*, which also
means to *"scourge to speak evil of one, slander, accuse falsely;
to mingle water and blood,"* (as when Jesus was speared in the
side as he hung on the cross and blood and water gushed out,
showing that he was losing his mana and life force).

The word "hang" as to hang on the cross, is *li*, in which the
root *li* (as *lili*) means *to hate, to abhor, to be filled with wrath,
to be jealous.* This repeats the things which make the low self
evil and which may also contaminate the middle self which
is strongly influenced by any low self emotion. Also described
are the evil things which obsessing spirits force upon the
lesser man when they gain power over him.

The mention of the crown of thorns is found only in John
19:1-5. "Thorn" is *kaka-laioa*, in which the root *kaka* means
to whip, this duplicating the idea of "scourge," which is *ha-
hau*, and which has a peculiar code meaning hidden in the
roots, for we know that *ha* stands for the entire process of accumulating mana, sending it to the High Self and presenting
the prayer for the thing desired. The root *hau* means *snow or
ice* and here the mana, as symbolized by "water" is shown
to be "frozen" so that it will not flow along the shadowy cord
to the High Self—a very graphic statement of the completely blocked path of Jesus as related in the story. The root *lai*
in the word given above for "thorn" means *to be silent*, and
this reinforces the idea that the prayer was impossible to
make effectively. (It also points to the obsession of the
"dumb" low self, as we have seen in our study of Isaiah, 53:7.)

Jesus died on the cross between two thieves. In the code
ai-hue is *thief*, and the literal meaning is *to steal food.* This is
the symbol of the evil spirits who fasten themselves on the

...m and live by stealing part of the mana made in the body. ...heir presence indicates the reason for the blocking of the path which caused the disaster for Jesus. One thief or spirit repented, and in this we have the information that the evil spirits can sometimes be reformed and made to leave.

The word for "death" is *make*, and one of its secondary meanings is to desire, while another is *to be made right, fitting and proper*. From this we see that death was not the end of everything for Jesus, but simply a delay in his evolutionary growth—this being the inborn desire or urge of humanity, no matter where in the evolutionary growth scale an individual may stand.

Jesus was laid in a "new tomb" or *hou ilina*, the "new" part having the code meaning of getting ready to start a new incarnation, after having met death. The word for "tomb," *i-lina*, has also the meaning of *to tighten or stretch, as a cord or rope*. This tightening is the Huna symbol of opening the shadowy cord or path and making it ready for use, in this case in the following life. The great stone which was rolled away from the tomb can be thought of as the total of the "stumbling blocks" which could not be removed on the cross, but which were cleared away before the next incarnation so that a clean slate might be provided for the next life. The evil spirits would leave at the death of their victim to find a new place to steal mana and have their evil urges shared by a living person.

The "resurrection" is *ala hou ana*, meaning from the root words, *to open the path anew*.

In order to understand better the dramatic lesson of the crucifixion, and to try to determine why Jesus became open to obsession, let us go back to the scene of the Passion. In John 17:1-5, we find a most significant piece of information. Jesus had been speaking to his disciples, and standing before them, he lifted his eyes unto the heavens and made this prayer: (The Fenton translation is used again.) "Father, the time has come! Perfect your Son, so that your son may magnify You; for You have invested Him with authority over all mankind in order that he may give eternal life to all whom You have intrusted to Him. And the eternal life is this: to obtain a knowledge of You the only true God, and the Messiah Whom You have sent. I have exalted You upon the earth by completing the work which You entrusted me to do. So now, Father, you restore Me to the honour which I had along with yourself before the world existed."

Not only do we see that Jesus, as the lesser man, was asking to be helped to take the final upward step, but he was counting his accomplishments boastfully before the listening disciples. This boastful attitude may be seen also in the following prayer made for the good of the disciples, and then in the prayer made for all believers, and finally, the prayer for the future of the believers.

As shocking as it is to consider his attitude boastful, when we have for so long been made by the outer teachings and the Church to believe that Jesus was God as a part of the Trinity, and so was perfect in every way from the beginning, the words of the prayers, if placed in the mouth of a modern religious leader, would at once identify him as a zealot and one afflicted with the arrogance of the smug, "better than thou" attitude. In the mouth of Jesus, the words are tolerable only if we accept him as an already perfect man and as a god and as part of the Trinity—a part which has been with the Father "from the foundations of the earth."

In the drama of his failure and crucifixion, which fills the long preliminary series of scenes, we see Jesus building up to the climax which will see the "heavens opening as a scroll" and himself elevated to a seat on the right hand of the Father. When the story opened, Jesus showed humility and gave the Father credit for all the "works" which he performed. Later he is made to identify himself more and more with the "Righteous Servant" of Isaiah, and so sure of himself did he become near the end that he dared to antagonize openly both the religious and political authorities of the day. It appears that only at the very end, after his betrayal, he began to doubt that the Last Day would arrive to save him and place him in the seat of honor.

If we understand the code of the betrayal correctly, it was at that time that his spiritual pride laid him open to obsession by certain spirits who were evil because they forced on him the emotions of pride which were their own besetting sins in life.

In his early ministry, Jesus taught that "the kingdom of

heaven is within." Nearing the end of his life, he sent the "seventy" out to preach the gospel with the promise that if they did so, the "Last Day" would arrive and all would reap a shining reward.

In Mark 14:61-62 we see the trend in this direction as we read, ". . . Again the high priest asked him, and said unto him, Art thou the Christ, the son of the Blessed? And Jesus said, I am: and ye shall see the Son of man sitting on the right hand of power, and coming in the clouds of heaven."

Jesus, early in his ministry, had roundly condemned the Jews who gave alms too openly and who made a pretense of righteousness when they voiced long prayers in public. At the end he had no alms to give, but his pride and the making of his prayer before his disciples was the very thing he had formerly condemned.

As the curtain falls on the last scenes of the drama of the crucifixion, all seems to be lost. The man who had learned to make himself "one with the Father," had been rendered impotent by evil spirits who had been able to obsess him and block his path. His weakness had been self-righteousness, the cardinal sin of the highest spiritual level. He had been held back by his desire to enjoy the fruits of his labors. He had not been content to have as his goal the final step in which he would have given up all thought of "me and mine."

He still desired to sit in glory on the right hand of the Father—at least that is what the Gospels and the code tell us.

But his expectations failed him. The inexorable tragedy counted off step by step. The skies did not unroll and there was no Last Day. They crucified him. And on the cross, the man who had worked miracles called on the Father for help, and his prayer was cut off—it was not delivered and not heard. He suffered the most agonizing of deaths.

What can be made of all this in terms of the code? Certainly not that Jesus, as a low-middle-self man, or as a triune man including his own High Self was forced by Ultimate God to lay down his life as a sacrifice or "ransom" for humanity. Only the lesser man is indicated in the "Son," and he clearly serves by generating and sending mana to the High Self. In terms of the code this is all—no other possible meaning. This allows the belated correction of one of the worst and most outstanding misconceptions to be found in Christianity. It turns us away from the angry and blood-thirsty Jehovah of the early Jews and gives us back the loving Father who, of course, is not Ultimate God, but always the High Self Father of Huna, whose love never fails or falters.

To the initiate or one familiar with the meaning of the code, the use of the cross as the symbol of all possible salvation by the Church contains an element of shuddering horror. The savagery of the constant worshipful contemplation of the image of the suffering and dying man in the very throes of utter failure, becomes more and more repulsive when it is realized that the drama did not end there—only paused.

Perhaps some day the cross will go and in its stead the emblem of the High Self will be used and venerated. This could be, as in ancient times in Egypt, the Sun, or it could be a single candle burning on a simple altar, representing the Light.

CHAPTER 7

The Temptation
And The Transfiguration

In a code-corrected version of the story of the life of Jesus, the temptation that came before he took up his ministry, comes in at this point. The authors of the Gospels were not at all hard pressed to handle the coded story. They switched events around as they saw fit, possibly the better to hide the secret truths from the ones "who were without."

The story continues, with Jesus in the tomb for three days, then coming again to life and meeting and talking to his disciples. Death has relieved him of the obsession which had bound him, for spirits leave one after death to go to find a living person to whom they can attach themselves and from whom they can draw mana to keep themselves hypnotically powerful and alive.

Having learned his lesson the hard way, Jesus now should go into the desert and fast for forty days and nights, be tempted by Satan himself, and be able to resist the offer of a position of power such as he had once dreamed of as a Messiah. Passing this test, he returns to his fellows, or should if the sequence were right, and goes to be given a final cleansing with water by John the Baptist.

Following this he should, in order to follow the pattern of the code, go into the new life that leads to the Transfiguration. However, the sequence is disrupted and we will have to insert at this place in our discussion the events that match the code.

In Matthew 17   and on, we have the story:

1. And after six days Jesus taketh Peter, James and John his brother, and bringeth them up into a high mountain apart. 2. And was transfigured before them: and his face did shine as the sun, and his raiment was white as the light. 3. And, behold, there appeared unto them Moses and Elias talking with him. 4. Then answered Peter, and said unto Jesus, Lord, it is good for us to be here: if thou wilt, let us make here three tabernacles; one for thee, one for Moses and one for Elias. 5. While he yet spake, behold, a bright cloud overshadowed them: and behold a voice out of the cloud which said, This is my beloved Son, in whom I am well pleased; hear ye him. 6. And when the disciples heard it, they fell on their face, and were sore afraid. 7. Jesus came and touched them, and said, Arise, and be not afraid. 8. And when they had lifted up their eyes, they saw no man, save Jesus only. 9. And as they came down from the mountain, Jesus charged them, saying, Tell the vision to no man, until the Son of man be risen again from the dead. (He had already risen from the dead in the proper code sequence of the story.)

Knowing now what the users of the code in the Gospels were at pains to try to pass on to future candidates for initiation through the code, let us see how they went about their task and with what success.

Perhaps the most important thing was to find words in the language of the code to fit their needs in undertaking this part of their task. In English the words they selected have only the outer meanings, but in the code the meanings are multiple and weighted with the greatest significance—as if, there being so few words to use, they must be of the finest and fullest.

"Transfiguration" is the first thing to inspect for hidden meanings. We must inquire into the nature of the Huna concept of this stage of man's progression and see how one set of meanings may interlock with others to complete the picture.

Hoo-pa-hao-hao is, *to be transfigured* or *to cause a change in appearance or to another form*. This fits the lines in Mark (3), "And was transfigured before them. And his raiment became shining, exceeding white as snow, so as no fuller on earth can whiten them." (The first interlocking of meaning comes with the mention of "raiment" which also means "robe," *kapa* and *lole lue-lue*, to which we will return later to see that the shadowy body was changed and glowed with white light.) The symbol of the High Self is "light" and it is sometimes seen in the physical sense as an intense white light which comes from no known source and which has in it no heat. We know from the mention of shining white light that the transfiguration must be a change in more than "appearance" or "form." The whole man has been changed, and into the only thing which shines with the amazingly white light, the High Self, housed in its robe or shadowy body.

If the correct sequence as indicated by the coded or secret story of the progress of Jesus and of his example for us to follow could be restored, we would, from the Transfiguration on, have a changed man. Now he becomes the gentle and loving Teacher who stands out in sharp contrast against the picture of the angry crusader who was making himself a place in the divine order and who angrily drove the money changers from the temple; and who cursed a fig tree because it bore no fruit. We leave behind us the polemics against the scribes and pharisees, and the belief that a place would be found to sit beside Jehovah and that the judgement of the Jews would be in his hands.

From the Transfiguration on, we should have the Savior we love, the gentle Jesus who loved children and preached the beautiful doctrine that "God is love". Here we have the man who yearned over his followers and promised them homes in "many mansions" and that he would send the "Comforter" after he was gone.

Now we have the real Christ, the anointed of the Father, who has his full contact with his High Self along the shadowy cord, and who, when making that contact can ask for help to perform miracles. In the other account of the earlier Jesus, we have him performing miracles, and must take it for granted that he was in that period able to make contact and heal, but that after his obsession and failure to meet the test of the Temptation, he temporarily lost the ability, especially when asking help for himself.

As long as Jesus considered himself the Messiah and believed that he was fulfilling the prophesies of Isaiah, and was about to usher in the Last Day, the term, Christ, does not well apply. The indiscriminate use of the title, Jesus Christ, has clouded the issue of his progress, and only the code can correct this misunderstanding.

It is interesting to see that the code word for "anoint" is *ha-mo*, which gives us the Ha Rite of prayer and also *to break, as the light of day*, and in this last meaning the full contact with the "Light" of the Father is stressed. The rite of annointment was used in early Egypt as a sacred mark of initiation, and for this purpose perfumed oils or greases were used. First came the baptism with water to wash away all sins, symbolically, and when this was done, the candidate was helped to open his path to the High Self. The anointing came as a confirmation of the full contact, and when the word passed into the Greek, it took on the meaning of one who was fully initiated, and was a title borrowed as the "Christ" when the story of Jesus was told. However, Jesus did not call himself a "Christ".

CHAPTER 8

The Last And Final Salvation

Scattered through the different versions of the Gospel story of the life of Jesus, the writers industriously inserted at various places the coded secret of secrets, that of the last step in human evolution or spiritual progress, in which man achieves UNION.

The knowledge of this last and greatest part of the hidden teachings spread with other items from the arcane lore, but no place did it get more attention or suffer more change and misinterpretation than in India, where the wonderful and final goal of life was the union of the man with the Ultimate God. Edward Arnold, in his "Light of Asia", expresses it beautifully in his words, "The dew drop slips into the shining sea." The man supposedly becomes blended with the vast field of consciousness that is God, and his identity is lost as he becomes one with God and becomes a part of God.

In the yoga writings the secret is not quite lost, and we have the integration of the lesser man as one soul who is, vaguely, a low and middle self, with his own High Self. But in it all, as in Paul's philosophy, the lower man was to be escaped from at all costs. It was the source of all darkness and remained a stumbling block until one could leave it behind and to its own sad devices while escaping to be pure and selfless and attain the longed-for union with the highest part of oneself—a part very badly misunderstood and the descriptions of which became much garbled.

The origin of the great secret lies obscured in the dim past, but as time went on, the wonderful truth took clearer coded form. In brief, it is this: The male and female were originally ONE, in the first human being, Adam, who was both male and female. Eventually, in the course of evolution, man was separated into the two sexes. At first he was the androgenous Adam of the creation story. But part of him was taken, in the form of a rib, and Eve was created to be his mate and to take on her specialized part in producing children and caring for them, releasing Adam for other endeavors.

In time, when life's lessons have been learned, possibly through a series of several incarnations, there comes the time when the middle self Adam, with his other half, Eve, evolve upward in the scale and "graduate" into the state of a High Self. As a High Self, they then blend in a UNION in which they have multiplied powers and intelligence, with the ability to see into the future to a limited extent, and with the mana received from the new lower selves over whom they assume charge, to make and remake events in answer to prayer.

This part of the hidden teaching gives us the climax of our lives and experiences. It offers wonderful beauty and satisfaction and enhanced abilities of all descriptions. It offers freedom at last from the body and its limitations, but still the connection of the shadowy cord to the lesser selves over whom we come to stand as guardian angels.

No dream of mankind is so nostalgic and filled with longing and frustrations as the dream of the perfect mate. It is the mate of the middle self "soul," and comes down to us as the greatly to be desired "Soul Mate", which has been so mistaken and so often ridiculed. This is the "marriage made in heaven". It comes at the end of lives of making war on the mate of the moment as we strive to force the partner into the mold of our dreams, and as we continually fail, for the final perfection is to be had and the great longing for perfect love is only to be realized in the ultimate state of UNION or blending—a state in which the male and female are freed of the defects shared with their physical bodies and the low self. At last the pure essence of their being can be expressed by the mates, and in the two halves of the sundered man we have the positive and negative joined. All internal strife is gone. The perfect love is there.

The hardest lesson of life may be that of learning to LOVE perfectly, unselfishly and without reservations. The low self is given to know this lesson imperfectly, but through the instincts. The mother loves her child, selfishly and possessively. The man loves his wife and children in the same blind way. But this is not the ideal love. It can turn to hate and work havoc in many lives. In the ultimate love, there is no turning back, no room for hate, all is cooperation and the joy of love is constant—a constant fulfillment.

Our Gospel Jesus, according to the code teachings, was all too busy at first to think of marriage. He was intent on being the Messiah, and love could wait. After the transfiguration we have the implied secret that he was ready for the "marriage made in heaven", but the story does not openly reach that beautiful ending. It stops just short of the point at which Jesues graduates to the High Self level, joins the Great Company of High Selves, and becomes the promised "Comforter".

The knowledge of the union of the male and female to make a new High Self is clearly presented in code in the early Christian writings which were not included when the canon was made up by the Church Fathers. More coded material is to be found in the literature which we have come to call "Gnostic."

One of the best sources of additional information is to be found in "The Gospel of Thomas," of which there have been a number of copies discovered in modern times. This book is very short and contains the sayings of Jesus rather than an account of his life and ministry. The author is said to have been the twin brother of Jesus and to have passed on to Matthias the sayings. The original was composed in Greek, and was translated later into the Egyptian language of the period, either Coptic or Sahadic.

In the same general period, with Alexandria in lower Egypt the center of such activities following a still earlier development of similar thought in Greece, the literature of the

"Gnosis" was written with many veiled meanings and used in the Mysteries of the time, probably as initiatory dramas. In the "Sayings" and in some of the gnostic writings we find almost identical passages dealing with the great secret of graduation to High Self level. Again the secret lore is found in sources farther afield, as in the writings belonging to the Mythraic Mysteries.

A good source book of this material is "FRAGMENTS OF A FAITH FORGOTTEN," by G.R.S. Mead, an English scholar of great learning and strong Theosophical leanings who wrote at the close of the last century.

From the Gospel of Thomas we have the passage, "When the Lord was asked by a certain man, When should his Kingdom come, He saith to him: When two shall be one, and the without be as the within, and the male with the female, neither male nor female."

A woman named Salome appears in some of this literature, either as a questioner or as one passing on information concerning the secret teachings. Here is a passage in which we have the one above more or less duplicated:

"When Salome asked how long should death hold sway, the Lord said unto her: So long as ye women bring forth; for I came to end the works of the female. And Salome said unto him: I have then done well in not bringing forth. And the Lord answered and said: Eat of every pasture, but of that which hath bitterness of death eat not. And when Salome asked when should these things of which she enquires be known, the Lord said: When ye shall tread upon the vesture of shame, and when two shall be one, the male with the female, neither male nor female."

In one translation a passage in the Gospel of Thomas reads, "Simon Peter says to them: Let Mary go out from our midst, for women are not worthy of life. Jesus says: See, I will draw her so as to make her male so that she may also become a living spirit like you males. For every woman who has become male will enter the Kingdom of heaven."

We also find a significant passage which reads, "Jesus said: Many stand outside at the door, but it is only the solitaries who enter into the bridal chamber."

These passages touch upon several things connected with the graduation. Salome is told that the time has come to stop bearing children and stop reincarnating or suffering physical death. This is, of course, the condition to be realized when one has evolved to the point of being ready to be united, as in Salome's case, with her male half, to make a new High Self which is no longer subject to physical death.

In the passage where Simon Peter wishes to have Mary put out of the group, we have what may have been the first sign of mistaken ideas in the outer version of the teachings. Much later, in the writings attributed to Paul, we have him taking much the same attitude. The Church, however, could not follow Paul in this putting away of women. The race has to be preserved through them. What Paul and others who abhorred marriage and intercourse with women missed entirely was the inner teaching that in the final incarnation the candidate for graduation draws away from all earthly ties of marriage and family, valuing the promised state of the High Self and desiring it greatly instead of the things of the physical and mental level which will be left behind.

One can only speculate as to the number of hermits who have become "solitaries" in the past because of their mistaken belief that this had something to do with winning salvation. "A little knowledge is a dangerous thing" says an old saw, and when we see the absurdities and misdirected efforts of the centuries, we can hardly avoid feeling that it was a very bad thing that the inner teaching of the code ever leaked out in the form which gave the outer teachings so many false directions.

A separation is to be experienced when one's middle and low selves are separated before graduation. Their two shadowy bodies must also be separated. During life and through the cycle of incarnations, the two shadowy bodies which house the two selves are connected and interblended, especially when in the physical body during the living periods. But as two garments are removed and one taken from the other, the shadowy bodies are separated. When the middle self, as a candidate, is ready to graduate, there is provided by the High Self a new garment which will clothe the united male and female selves as one unit, not as two.

This shadowy-substance garment is called in some texts the "Robe of Glory," in others the "Robe of Light," and when it houses the High Self it gives out white light which is seen on rare occasions by lesser men on the physical level. The "seamless" robe or garment is the symbol of the single shadowy body of a High Self, also of the united male and female selves living in it. In the crucifixion scene, the code is used to show that the man, Jesus, on the cross was not a High Self. He was stripped of his robe, and we read, John 19:23–24,

"Then the soldiers, when they had crucified Jesus, took his garments, and made four parts, to every soldier a part; and also his coat. Now the coat was without a seam, woven from the top throughout. They therefore said among themselves, Let us not rend it, but cast lots for it, whose it shall be."

The changing of the shadowy bodies or garments ties in closely with the idea of transfiguration in the code word for "garment," this being *lole*, which also means, *to alter from one thing to another* and *to rectify*. Thus we see that the final *making perfect* includes the correcting of any faults and the changing from one self level to the next, the shadowy body also being changed in some way. That the low self also steps up a level is indicated in the roots *lo* and *le*, the first meaning *the brain of the person or animal* and referring in the older usage of the language to the seat of intelligence in the intestines, this being a sure indication that the low self was meant. The second root has the meaning of *to leap or fly upward*, and so gives us the upward progression to the next level at the time of graduation, when all three of the selves of the man play their parts.

The idea of going up a step is found in the coded phrase, "to tread upon the garment of shame." "Tread" is *hele*, which has the same *le* root and which also means *to pass on*, or in this case, *"pass on a step higher."* "Shame" is *hila-hila*, which gives in the root *hi*, *to droop; to be weak*, and *la*, *light*. As the shadowy bodies are worn out they may be said to become "weak," and to lack "light," which we know is also "life" in terms of the code. From another angle we may say that with the low and middle selves, during their cycle of incarnations, they become tired and weak in contrast with the High Self which remains ever the same. The "garment of shame" can only refer to the lower selves and the animal nature which must be cleansed and made ready for the upward step. Adam and Eve may be said to have put on the first "garment of shame" when they were placed in bodies and came to know that they were naked. Not until they could, after many incarnations, put off those bodies of flesh and reunite as a High Self could they rise above the level of the lesser man who knows shame.

In one of the Sayings we have the word "mingled" used instead of "shame." We read, "There is a mingling that leadeth to death, and there is a mingling which leadeth to life." Here we have the sex union on the lower levels where death ends each incarnation and the mingling or uniting effort is left incomplete. But at the time of graduation the mingling of the male and female results in a continuing life beyond physical death. The code word for "mingle" is *kaa-wili*, in which the root *kaa* has a secondary meaning of *a cross*. *Wili* is *to writhe in pain*. The code intimation seems to be that all efforts to complete the lesser union on the level of the incarnating selves results in pain because of the lack of "perfection."

One of the gnostic fragments dealing with the union of the male and female selves is to be found starting on page 74 of Mead's small book, THE WEDDING SONG OF WISDOM.

From the translation of the ritual we read, "For this is the Mystery of the gate of Heaven, and this is the house of God, where the Good God dwells alone; into which house no impure man shall come—but it is kept under watch for the Spiritual alone; where, when they come, they must cast away their garments, and all become Bridegrooms, obtaining their true Manhood through the Virginal Spirit."

The "Virginal Spirit" is the female half of the pair about to graduate. She is "virginal" in the sense of being purified of all earthly things which do not belong on the high level where physical generation has ended. The male completes his "manhood" only by adding to himself her "womanhood." Together they reap the promised reward of the hundred times greater mental and mana powers belonging to the High Selves. (See THRICE GREATEST HERMES, i. 180, 181.)

Sophia represents the "Virginal Spirit" in some of the gnostic literature. After graduation, or the "marriage made in heaven," she becomes the Holy Ghost or Mother half of the Father-Mother High Self.

Mead tells us on pages 75 through 78 of the ritual of the "Sacred Marriage," as given on page 50 of THE HYMN OF JESUS, in which Sophia, as the candidate for initiation says:

(1) "I would be wounded (or pierced)." In an alternate Latin translation it reads, "I would be dissolved" (that is) "by consuming love."

(2) "I would be begotten."

(3) "I would be adorned."

(4) "I would be at-oned."

These four statements of desire and intention cover the ground of graduation, and in the first we meet again the need to suffer in order to be cleansed. There is still something veiled in this matter, however. Jesus, when crucified, was pierced in the side by a spear to bring about his death. That is the outer meaning, and death seems to be presented by the writers as the final disaster when one is cut off from one's High Self. But the word *hou*, for "pierce," also means *new; repeat; do again*, and is the code symbol for being born again in a fresh incarnation. In the case of the candidate for graduation, the death of the middle self, so to speak, is to make possible its rebirth into the Kingdom of Heaven or the High Self state.

Also, in the matter of the desire to be "pierced" we note that the word "side" is *ao-ao* in the code, with a secondary meaning of *to enlighten, to escape, and a new way or course of life*. All of these meanings apply well to the things desired by the candidate, perhaps as a result of the suffering of the cleansing to make him "perfect." Certainly, the rebirth into the High Self level ushers the middle self into an entirely new way of life, and a way of vastly greater enlightenment.

The Latin translation of "be dissolved" fits well the idea of the doing away with the shadowy body and the separation from the low self to make possible what is to come. "By consuming love" would suggest that in the love of the mates in the new union the very power of the love consumes the unwanted things left behind. The old middle selves, male and female, are "consumed" and their substance and very being enters into the formation of the new High Self.

The second desire, "I would be begotten," repeats the idea of rebirth into the level of the High Self. "To beget" is the code symbol of bringing about a birth or a rebirth. "Beget" is *hoohua* in the language of the code, and means *to bring forth, as a female* or to be born.

The desire to "be adorned" is simple to understand, now that we have learned the meaning of the "robe of light," which is the shadowy body of the newly united pair—this union being plainly stated as the great desire in, "I would be at-oned."

Mead comments on the desire for "at-one-ment," saying, "We now approach the Mystery of Union, when the soul abandons with joy its separateness and frees itself from the limitations of its 'possessions'—of that which is 'mine' as apart from the rest. Enough has now been given to assure the reader that the Sacred Marriage was a fundamental mystery with the Christian Gnostics."

A slightly longer, and very similar invocation or expression of desire is given by Mead in his booklet, MYTHRAIC RITUAL, page 33. We read:

"Hail Lord, Thou Master of the Water!

"O Lord, being born again, I pass away in being made Great, and having been made Great, I die.

"Being born from out the state of birth-and-death that giveth birth to mortal lives, I now, set free, pass to the state transcending birth as Thou hast stablished it, according as Thou hast ordained and made the Mystery."

This covers well the matter of the death of the old middle self as it is helped to perfection by the use of the grace and power of the High Self. The title, "Master of the Water" is Huna in that the High Self is the master of the high mana which can be used to produce miracles and to bring about the union of graduation.

There are several passages in the Gospels which repeat the work of the initiatory degree of the "marriage made in heaven," and some of these lead up to the final stages in which the Union is shown as completed in the transfiguration.

In Matthew, Chapter 19, we have a passage already mentioned as having caused much misunderstanding in outer circles, so that men became hermits and castrates in the hope of gaining entrance into the Kingdom of Heaven. In verses 11 and 12 we read, "But he said unto them, All men cannot receive (understand the inner meaning of) this saying, save those to whom it is given. For there are some eunuchs, which were so born from their mother's womb: and there are some eunuchs, which were made eunuchs of men: and there be eunuchs, which have made themselves eunuchs for the kingdom of heaven's sake. He that is able to receive it, let him receive it."

The translators of the New Testament in yesterday's Hawaii, may have felt that the Hawaiian word for "eunuch" was not sufficiently descriptive to be used, so they worked over the English word and used it in the text as "eunuha," which lost for it the whole of the code significance. The word *ma-hu* contained the code, but did not mean a castrate, it meant an individual of both sexes, a hermaphrodite. The root *ma* means *to accompany* or may be used as a "formative" root, and in this case with the root *hu*, which means *to rise up*, we have *to accompany someone and cause a rising up*. This is most obscure except to the ones able to "receive" it.

We have just watched a degree scene acted out in which the woman is depicted as the "virgin" and as the mate ready for the "marriage." Here we have the male, also in a state of progression in which he has left the world and the work of procreation to become a symbolic eunuch. The barren female and the sterile male have become free from all lesser desires and wish only for the final Union.

This sterile condition is beautifully presented in the story by having the little children brought for Jesus to bless and he says, ". . . for of such is the kingdom of heaven." He was not speaking of the children as the "little angels" we have with us when fond parents present to visitors most unlikely offspring. He was speaking in veiled terms of their lack of reproductive powers and activities.

There is an obscure word familiar to the kahunas, but which does not have the meaning of "eunuch," but which applied precisely to the Union of the mates. It is *ko-ko-hu*, which means *to have a form; to take the garb or assume the manners of another.* This word is used to describe the *ma-hu* or hermaphrodite. The code meaning of "to have a form" covers the full range of the Union in so far as the new shadowy body is concerned—this being the new "garb" or "body of light" to be put on by the new High Self. The "to assume the manners of another" touches on the very depths of the secret concerning the state in which the mates become One.

We cannot have this state of splendid love and Light explained to us too often. The candidate must be helped to understand that in this blending and union of the mates, nothing is given up—nothing. Nothing is lost: all is gained. The male retains all of his treasures of maleness, and so does the female her treasures. But each is blessedly permitted to annex a whole world of sensibilities and powers owned by the other and developed through the toils of several lives. There is nothing to lose, and ALL to gain—with the magnificent bonus of the perfect love that no longer has "the naked sword that lies between thee and me" of the physical low self and the opinionated middle self.

In the new state of oneness there is no longer the necessity to form opinions from possibly faulty information. The new High Self identifies itself with the thing to be known, and is able to know the exact truth about it. At last there is the realization of the meaning of the cryptic saying, "Ye shall know the truth, and the truth shall make you free." The code word for "free" is *kuu-wale*, which also means from the two roots *to be released* and enabled *to enter a state of being without qualifications* or the usual limitations belonging to the mental limitations of the two lesser selves.

While the Book of Revelations is not too clear in its code implications, there are parts of it which fit in simple symbology the Union which is the goal and end of the life cycle. In 21:2-5, we read, "And I John saw the holy city, the new Jerusalem, coming down from God out of heaven, prepared as a bride adorned for her husband. (The pair ready for the marriage which is made in heaven may be symbolized here.) . . . And God shall wipe away all tears from their eyes; and there shall be no more death, neither sorrow, nor crying, neither shall there be any more pain: for the former things are passed away. (The new High Self is to be set free of the things which trouble the lesser pair of selves, even of the need for physical death.) And he that sat upon the throne said, Behold, I make all things new . . .''

Continuing with this provocative comparison of the ''bride'' and the new Jerusalem, in verse 9, we select bits to apply to the central thesis of Union. ''. . . Come hither, I will shew thee the bride, the Lamb's wife. . . . And had a wall great and high, and had twelve gates (perhaps the needed number of incarnations to reach the time of Union) . . . and three gates. . . .'' (Perhaps standing for the three selves and their progression through the series of incarnations until all three graduate to a next higher level. The ''Lamb's wife'' may suggest his mate in graduation.)

One can but wonder whether the writer of the Revelations had in mind the same ''grace'' as had the kahunas who believed that only by the ''grace'' of the High Self can the middle self be made ''perfect'' and ready for Union. At any rate, the writer ends his book with the lines, ''The grace of our Lord Jesus Christ be with you all.'' And we know that in the code version of the Gospels, Jesus became a Christ, but only after taking the great upward step into the Kingdom.

In Polynesia, where the early kahuna beliefs and practices survived down to modern times in a surprisingly good state of preservation, the kahunas reared families and at the same time acted as healers or leaders in various fields of endeavor. Judging from their attitude toward life and inner growth, we may safely conclude that anyone who wishes to try for graduation at the end of the present incarnation can do no better than to live the hurtless, kindly and unselfish life which is the mark of the candidate who has become ready to move on and up.

The secret of secrets, that of the ''soul mates'' who will eventually be united, need not worry the candidate for graduation. Wherever he or she may be in the world, makes little difference. The High Self will take care of the work of finding the mate and bringing about the Union at the proper time. For the candidate, the real and pressing task and necessity is to learn to love as greatly and as unselfishly as possible. The mate may be in the home or the vicinity, or may be in some other land, or even waiting as a spirit. We have no way to know the mate even should we meet him or her, or even if married to one who seems less than perfect because still a middle and low self on the physical level where the lovely perfections are not yet to be realized.

One High Self, being a combination of male and female, is in charge of the two halves of the Adam, and is looking after the Eve, no matter where she may be during the long period of growth and experience which prepares them for the final Union. It is very possible, so we may suppose, for the two mates to meet and love in one or more lives. This would be most desirable, but even if long separated by time or circumstances, the bridge is love—the deep and instinctive and enduring love which is the dream of men and women the world over. In any case, when the time is ripe, the High Selves will bring them together, if only at the time of their graduation.

CHAPTER 9

Summary

As a summary, let us consider what Jesus taught to those in the outer circle. To begin with, he did not say that he was of the line of David. That was added by others. He did not say that his mother was a virgin or that she had conceived him through a miraculous contact with the Holy Spirit. He taught at first that he was the embodiment of the Messiah as described in Isaiah's prophecies, that the world was about to come to an end and that the heavens would unroll like a scroll and that he would sit in the place of honor on the right hand of God and judge the Jews. He never retracted his statements on that score, but the Resurrection came to cancel it, even though many still expect the Last Day to come at any minute.

Jesus taught that love was the "greatest of these things." He taught us not to hurt others, but to "love one's neighbor as oneself." He gave veiled instructions as to how to pray, which did little to change the older way. He instituted the "Lord's Supper," but made it only a rite of remembrance which was out of place before the Crucifixion because he still thought that the end of the world was at hand and he would be glorified. He washed the feet of the disciples, but few followers took this to heart and made a rite of it.

He taught that there was "The Father," and that prayers should be directed to Him. He taught that the ancient system of blood sacrifice should be given up, but did not explain to "those without" what should take its place. At no time did he call himself a Christ, although he said that he and the Father were "one." He taught a vague doctrine of immortality and of resurrection, with heaven or hell as a reward or punishment. He did not say that breaking the man-made, or church rules of ritual worship was a sin.

Paul and others misunderstood the Gospels and, because they did not have knowledge of the inner teachings, invented mistaken doctrines which were accepted by the early Church. Among these was the doctrine that Jesus had to be sacrificed on the cross to redeem mankind from the "sins of Adam." Paul belittled women and gave them a place far down the scale of life.

The doctrine of the Trinity was slowly evolved. In it God was divided into three equal parts or gods. The idea was grounded in ancient pre-Christian religions, and was a bad misconception. It failed to cover the trinity of the three selves of man—the low, middle and High.

The INNER TEACHINGS gave us the correct method of making a prayer and taught that miraculous results could be had from such appeals to the Father. They told who and what the Father was. The example set by Jesus taught us to be humble and not let our contact with the High Self be broken lest we be crucified, symbolically. The secret of the Transfiguration and of graduation, to be followed by UNION, was stressed. Love and the hurtless and helpful life was given us as the prime example of the good and normal life—the normal family life. Nothing was taught that even hinted that a belief in Jesus as the savior from the sins of Adam was necessary, and no priest was *recommended* to act as an intercessor with God and to dole out forgiveness or withhold it. The duty of a teacher was to heal or to cast out obsessing spirits and help one get the path to the High Self unblocked. Nor was any form of Church given authority to exercise authority over those who worshiped the Father in spirit and in truth. It was taught that every individual was accountable only to his High Self and his fellow men. He needed no Sacraments.

* * * * * * * * * * * *

And so the breaking of the code gives us back our original Lord, Jesus, the Master of the Ha Rite, the teacher of the secret of effective prayer, the one who set the great example with his own life and who became a "Christ." He taught of the Way, the Truth and the Light, and stands now before us in a new guise.

We can exult with the Voice in Revelations that cries, "Behold, I make all things new." But we recall, "He who hath ears, let him hear," and "Many are called and few are chosen."

THE END

APPENDIX A

The Mystery Of The Father

The English and Greek languages, with which we have to deal in the New Testament as it has been handed down to us, are very faulty from the point of view of the code. For instance, we have no really adequate word for the "Father", as used by the initiates.

In the language of the code, however, we have an excellent and descriptive word in *aumakua*. But to the missionaries this was a heathen word, and they would have none of it. They took the root, *makua*, which means earthly "parents", capitalized it and used it for "Father".

The full word *aumakua* begins with the root *au*, which means a *self*, and translates, *Time Parent*, or *one of much greater* age. Even the kahunas kept secret the real meaning of the word, and let it be known that the "Father" was a chief or other great person who, after death, had become deified to some extent.

But one self or person cannot become a parent. IT TAKES TWO, a male and a female. But when the middle self Adam UNITES with the middle self Eve, they no longer produce children. They cease to have sex in the sense of the word as we use it. The term "Father" could as well have been "Mother", but the initiates thought of the High Self as "Father-Mother". In it we find all the characteristics of the male as well as of the female, but the kindness and love and understanding is much greater than on the level of the lower man.

The "kingdom of heaven" uses the word *au-puni* for "kingdom", and the first root, *au*, is the Mother-Father, while the root, *puni*, has but one meaning, that of *a place*. So we have the hidden meaning of THE PLACE OF THE FATHER-MOTHER. This is a place of LIGHT, and all of our struggles and endeavors lead upward to that place or kingdom of Light.

"Heaven", in the code is *la-ni* and we know that *la* is the High Self. The root *ni*, as we have seen in *ni-ni* has the meaning of *to pour out, as grain*, and this takes us back to the "bowl" symbol of the Egyptians, in which the grain is poured from the bowl as a glyph meaning the blessings of the Higher Being.

In the Egyptian "Book of the Dead" as found in various tombs, we find that the man always arrives in heaven with his loved wife. In the pictures painted on the tomb walls we see the man accompanied by his wife entering *"amenta"* or heaven.

As there is nothing definite in the Gospels to tell us of the love life of Jesus, we can only speculate. Martha or Mary may have originally been coded as his mate, but in becoming ready to graduate with him into a Parental Spirit, we could not have had her still married and bearing children. She had, like Salome in the quotations already given, ceased to bear—was "barren" or *pa*, in the code, the meaning of which, in addition to *barren*, is *to cause one thing to approach or touch another*, and in this we see the coming together of the barren pair, as middle selves (who lack physical bodies for producing offspring), to blend into one (still barren) High Self. And, lest we mistake the true meaning of the word, it has also the very significant translation of *a pair*, and we see the paired or mated selves being brought together for the graduation or union.

But the parental love of the Father-Mother is not lost when the pair blends to make a new *Aumakua*. The love abides and of this we can be happily sure. We are being watched over and helped and guided in every way that our actions and the law of "free will" allows. We cannot be forced into a better way of life. That is against what seems to be a divine law. We must be allowed to learn by experience, and it is not until we come to know that the High Self is there, and that we can appeal to it to take its very helpful part in living our lives, can we know the blessedness of such help.

In many ancient religions the Mother is recognized in a way. She becomes the Mother Goddess, as in Isis who is the mate of Osiris and mother of Horus, in Egypt. She is the one to whom people prayed when needing love and understanding of the mothering kind. In Christianity the Father was, at least in the outer doctrines, too much like the severe and vengeful Jehovah, so people soon were praying to Mary, mother of Jesus, and as all prayers can go only to the High Self, there were answers forthcoming. Soon Mary was a dear part of the divine family, even if she had no place in the Trinity and even if the Pauline inventions had thrown a dark taboo over all that was feminine. Only in recent years was Mother Mary freed from the very lowly state of the temptress female in Christianity and officially canonized as a saint. It is strange to hear Saint Mary still called "mother of God" in the Church rituals, and when we know the inner teachings of Jesus, we also know that Jesus was never a God or even a part of a divine Trinity. He was first of all a man, and as the decoded Gospels now tell us, he never became more than a High Self Father-Mother.

Above the High Self level of being, we are told that there are levels and levels, always moving higher, until at the very top is Ultimate God—whose nature is so beyond human conception that we can never know Him except in the image reflected around us, first in a vast Universe, and last, in the plants and animals around us—all growing in orderly fashion under what we can only call a "law" and with the guidance of something we call "instinct" for want of a better and more explanatory word.

We know so very little. But the knowledge handed down to us by the initiates who have gone on before, becomes all the more precious as we search for the "real truth" (*oioia*).

THE MYSTERY OF THE NAME

The early Egyptians made much of the NAME of a god or devil or man. The "name", *ren*, was counted by Budge and some other writers on their religious beliefs as one of the several elements that made up the man. It was counted with the three selves or spirits, the three shadowy bodies or doubles, the three grades of vital force or mana. But it was not really a part of the man. Instead, it was a part of the outer doctrine or of the Egyptian practice of magic in which spells were recited, gods and devils invoked or driven away and amulets were used with names inscribed on them for protection or luck.

Like many such things, the belief became a superstition hard to eradicate. In Isaiah, 55:13, he ends a rhapsodical chapter describing the good days to come when the rule of the Lord shall take over and sin be banished. We read,

"Instead of the thorn shall come up the fir tree, and instead of the briar the myrtle tree, and it shall be to the Lord for a name, for an everlasting sign that shall not be cut off."

We have already seen the code significance of "thorn" and know that the hidden meaning is "to break" the contact along the shadowy cord with the High Self. Isaiah promises that this shall not happen again but it is not clear just what magic he thought might lie in the "name" to be given the Lord or just how it could serve as an everlasting "sign" that the line of contact along the "path" would not again be blocked. He was, evidently, thinking of the state of one who graduates into the estate of a High Self. A little light on his intention is thrown by his code use of the word for "sign" (or, as we find it used in John 14:48, "wonders") it is *ku-pai-a-na-ha*, the root meanings of which give us *to send away by water*, pointing to the prayer thought forms sent with the flow of mana (water) to the High Self, and in the familiar root *ha* the whole mechanism of prayer. Perhaps this tells us that when we learn to pray correctly, we shall see "signs and wonders" which will PROVE that the work is being done by the Lord, or Father-Mother Self.

It may be that the writers of the Gospels and of Revelations thought they could make the outer teachings of the account they wrote all the more acceptable to the "ones who were without" by using a form of superstition with which they were long familiar. Evidently the people of the day were accustomed to use the Egyptian way of calling on a name or pronouncing a name as a part of their magic. The Egyptians believed that if you knew the name of a god or devil, you could pronounce it and then recite your incantation, forcing that entity to obey or give what was asked. In the "Book of the Dead" the spirit of the dead man was supplied with the names of all the demons who stood blocking the many gates to heaven. He had only to call the name of each as he approached and they would be forced to allow him to pass through.

The individual was often supplied with a secret name known only to himself and one parent, and he guarded it against being discovered and used to conjure him.

In Revelations, 3:12, we read, "Him that overcometh will I make a pillar in the temple of my God, and he shall go no more out: and I will write upon him the name of My God, and the name of the city of my God, which is the new Jerusalem, which cometh down from out of heaven from my God: and I will write upon him my new name." And in 2:17 we read, "He that hath an ear, let him hear what the Spirit saith unto the churches; To him that overcometh will I give to eat of the hidden manna (mana), and will give him a white stone, and in the stone a new name written, which no man knoweth save him that receiveth it."

Here we have numerous code words which already have been discussed, but it is evident that the one spoken of is the successful candidate who had come to the place where he is ready to graduate into the kingdom of heaven or High Self level. But the accustomed use of the "name" is also to be seen, and we are assured that the new and transfigured candidate will be given a new and very secret name.

The "white stone" in which the new name is to be written is a play on words in order to use the code. "White," *kea*, is the cross of the crucifixion, reminding the one addressed that this test has been finished with. "Stone" is *po-ha-ku*, the root *po* reminding us of the *darkened condition*; the root *ha* of the *enlightened condition* when one has learned to make the correct prayers, *to raise up*, or send the mana and prayer to the Father-Mother. The writer's intention can hardly be missed, once one has become acquainted with the code.

In several places in the Gospels the instructions are given

"ask in my name", and while this conforms nicely to the outer teachings, it means little to the inner teachings. "MY NAME", we see, never means the name of Jesus as the man, but the Transfigured or Christed Jesus who is the High Self. It is the Father-Mother who is appealed to in prayer and on whose "name" we must call.

The classic example is at the end of the Lord's Prayer, where for centuries good Christians have finished the prayer with, "We ask it in Jesus' name. Amen." The "Amen" is a corruption of the name of the great god Ammon, of early Egypt. He was worshipped by the masses while Osiris, Iris and Horus, as the Divine Trinity were worshipped by others, especially the more instructed. The evil Egyptian god Set was the original Devil and may have been intended in the lines, ". . . and deliver us from evil or the evil one." (The Revised Version uses "the evil one" as the correct translation.)

The prayer was not original with Jesus, but is paraphrased on its older forms long in use by the Jews, and may well be one borrowed from the Egyptians.

THE MYSTERY OF NIRVANA

It may be of interest to some to know that the belief in the graduation from the middle self level to that of the High Self was known in India and taught by Gautama, who was a prince of the land but who renounced his high place in life and later was given the title of "Buddha," in much the same way that Jesus was given the title of "Christ." The period was several hundreds of years earlier than the appearance of Jesus, which tends to show the antiquity of the idea.

Buddhism was a reform movement, just as Christianity was a contradiction of the old ideas of the Jews. Prince Gautama, who later was given the title of "Buddha," or "An Enlightened One," accepted the belief in the endless succession of incarnations and the burdensome Law of Karma. He also accepted the belief of Yoga that there was a way to escape "being broken on the wheel." But he refused to be deeply involved in the endless speculations concerning the real and the unreal.

From the great similarity of the system which he evolved, in comparison to that embodied in the coded Christian teachings, we can only conclude that he, also, had some access to Huna.

It is impossible at this late date to learn from the Buddhist scriptures what inner doctrines might have been known and taught to the "elect" of Gautama's day. The tradition of an inner or "esoteric" doctrine is accepted by a great many students, much as has the tradition of a mystery teaching in Christianity.

Whatever knowledge Gautama came to have, he used it in making his new religious system. In the outer teaching he held that men and women should follow the "Middle Path" or way of life, doing the things necessary to normal living but taking care to hurt no one. The Golden Rule was preached, and the promise held out that in due time such kindly living would help one to "escape the wheel."

Shortly before the writing of the "Sayings" of Jesus or the enlarged account of his life—to say nothing of the Mystery writings, Gnosis and initiatory dramas current at the beginning of the Christian era—Gautama was teaching his version of "graduation." As it has come down to us in the surviving outer teachings of Buddhism, he taught that one could leave the illusionary lower world and enter a special state which was called "Nirvana." This is a Sanskrit word which means "to stop blowing." It suggests the ceasing of physical breathing and so the extinction of physical life. The escape was likened to the "blowing out of a candle"—leaving nothing—an extinction.

This was a very strange doctrine in that it failed to provide the needed motives for trying to enter Nirvana. All that it offered was relief from the much emphasized pain of living and dying. At least that is all that has come down to us in the Buddhist Scriptures. On the other hand, judging from what Gautama actually did during his ministry, we cannot avoid the conclusion that to the ones near him he must have taught something very similar to the Huna theory of graduation.

Gautama gathered around him a band of disciples who may well be compared with the "elect" of Jesus. He formed them into a brotherhood of "Sanga," and taught them that in order to attain the Nirvanic state they should give up all desire for the things of ordinary life. They were to give up all possessions and all attachments to family and friends. They were to get rid of all obligations and put on the yellow robe of the outcasts. Thus identifying themselves as pilgrims bent on wending their holy way to Nirvana, they became homeless vagabonds, begging daily for food to sustain them.

In this respect, the disciples of Jesus were almost as extreme. They did not put on distinctive garb, but they stopped working and lived on charity.

In the beginning, both Buddhist and Christian systems were confined to a certain "chosen" few. But in both, the inner teaching soon became lost and the masses invaded the ranks of the "elect." In Christianity the hermits flourished and monasteries and nunneries grew with great rapidity. In India, after the death of Gautama, a mass movement seems to have arisen and crushed out the inner teachings, for men and women broke all caste restrictions and, rich and poor, including a king or two, took the yellow robe. Rich men gave their fine homes and grounds to the Sanga or Brotherhood, and princes their palaces and gold. It became a very easy way of life and very attractive. The trouble was that it was contrary to all the rules of social progress. Men and women refused to bring up families or to produce things for the support of communal life. It was inevitable that the strange structure should be forced to change or fall. In India the ruling Brahman caste made war on the new religion so energetically that many of the faithful were driven out, but did missionary work in far places. Changes took place. The call to try to enter Nirvana became mingled with the more practical call to work and to meet obligations. But the good and kindly way of life of the "Noble Eight Fold Path" or "Middle Way" was preserved, just as the more practical side of Christianity was later preserved.

The older beliefs of India, which antedated Buddhism, had far less influence on Christianity than the monasticism of the "Sanga" organized by Gautama. But in time the older Hinduism, especially the Brahmanistic priesthood and its powers, came to furnish an example upon which the Papal structure of the early Church was fashioned.

While Christianity became dogmatized and contaminated by borrowings from other beliefs, it was saved from the caste system and the folly of too much karma and too endless a series of reincarnations. This was due to the fact that in the Gospels those items, against which Guatama had revolted, had never been markedly present.

Christianity, once its basic patterns had been rather completely set, by about the year 400 A.D., became fixed, and, in a static condition, droned on and on through the Dark Ages. In India, during this long period, Buddhism was stamped out by the Brahmans and the cruel caste system was enforced, with the priests at the top and the outcasts at the bottom of the religio-social scale.

Illustrations
of Ancient Symbols

Early Egyptian hieroglyphic sign for GRASSHOPPER: The symbol for the subconscious part of mind. It makes the vital force or mana for all three "selves" or spirit parts of the man.

Plate No. 1

Glyph for BEE: the symbol of the conscious mind part or "self" of the man. It takes the mana from the subconscious and sends it along the shadowy cord to the Super-conscious Self. The symbol for this mana is "honey"—which became the "Ambrosia" or favorite drink of the Greek gods.

Plate No. 2

The SCARAB BEETLE, which with the SUN was the symbol of the Super-conscious Part of mind. It was assigned creative power.

Plate No. 3

The SUN was the symbol of the Super-conscious Self. Its symbol was "light", or "RA" in the Egyptian. "La" in Hawaiian. Sun worship was the outer form but not the secret form of worship.

Plate No. 4

This BIRD was the symbol standing for any of the three "selves" of the man.

Plate No. 5

The THREE SELVES of man were symbolized by three birds interlocking to show the close association of the three spirit parts of the man.

Plate No. 6

The glyph for WATER was made up of three lines of waves to symbolize the three grades of vital force or mana used by the three selves. They were the mesmeric, the hypnotic and the miracle force of the three selves and were very important to the understanding of the secret system and its use.

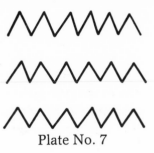

Plate No. 7

The seal or name of an ancient pharaoh who was considered divine. The three pairs of uplifted arms symbolize the THREE DOUBLES or 'shadowy' bodies of the three selves. The uplifted arms symbolize the part the bodies of the lower selves play in sending the prayer "seeds" to the sun which is above and which represents the Highest of the three selves.

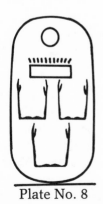

Plate No. 8

The umbrella, which casts a shadow, is a second symbol for the shadowy body or double.

Plate No. 9

The cord or thread, made of shadowy body substance and invisible, was so important that it appears in several glyph forms.

The cord with nnnnnnnnnn

Plate No. 10

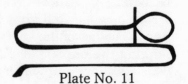

The cord with three bends representing the path over which the prayer travels with a flow of mana (water). It means "offering".

Plate No. 11

The cord with a knot in it, representing the blocked path that does not reach the High Self.

Plate No. 12

The cord in three loops representing the part each of the three shadowy bodies must play in making the effective prayer.

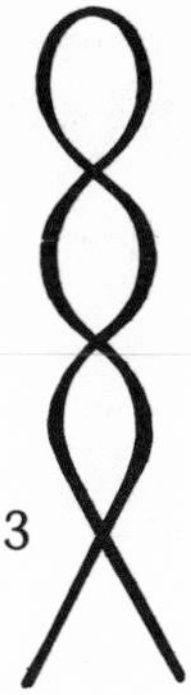

Plate No. 13

The arm, laid across the three shadowy bodies symbolizes "power", as represented in the perfect prayer that gets results.

Plate No. 14

The Superconscious Self as a lesser god holding its end of the shadowy cord which leads up from the low and middle selves.

Plate No. 15

A bowl. The glyph for "Lord" and symbolizing the High Self.

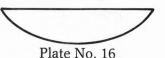

Plate No. 16

The bowl turned sidewise to pour out seeds which represent the "seeds" or thought forms of the prayer when materialized and made real as the answer to a prayer.

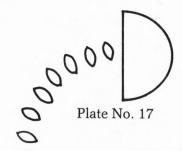

Plate No. 17

The feather, symbolizing "truth". Against it was weighed the heart of each dead person to see if he had lived a proper life.

Plate No. 18

The glyph for "breath" was a sail. Breath entered into the very important work of accumulating extra mana to send to the High Self. (Glyph No. 11 symbolized the use of mana as "power.")

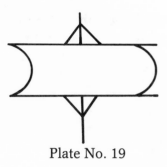

Plate No. 19

The seal or name of the god Amen, in whose name favors were asked from the gods for centuries. We still end our prayers by repeating his name, "Amen."

Plate No. 20

The Egyptian symbol of Life.

Plate No. 21

The glyph meaning "beloved." As an amulet it was worn as a collar.

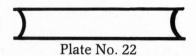

Plate No. 22

The glyph for the amulet worn by gods and men. From the glyph for "beloved" is suspended a heart divided into two parts with a line, but joined. It means "union," and signifies the hope for the final union with the mate. The "beloved" sign made a collar to fasten around the neck, and, oddly enough, the gods are pictured usually with the heart hanging from the collar in the back.

Plate No. 23

The glyph for the thorn. The symbol of the fixations or "eating companions."

Plate No. 24

For information about the author, write to:

Hunā Research Inc.
1760 Anna Street
Cape Girardeau. MO 63701-4504
USA